Jeremy Sherman

**Evolving Press
Berkeley, CA**

Copyright 2003 by Evolving Press

Published by Evolving Press
editor@evolvingpress.com

Sherman, Jeremy E.
Negotiate with yourself and win! Doubt management skills for people who can
hear themselves think./by Jeremy Sherman

Negotiate with yourself and win!

Doubt management skills for people who can hear themselves think.

Jeremy Sherman

Jeremy Sherman

Dedication

To my teachers, one and all; advertent and inadvertent, affirming and critical, influencing me with live demonstrations of good, bad and interesting ways to handle doubt, those who lectured and those who listened while I taught and thought out loud.

Especially to Evolutionary Neurobiologist Terry Deacon, mentor extraordinaire.

The test of a first-rate intelligence is the ability to hold two opposed ideas in mind at the same time and still retain the ability to function.'

F. Scott Fitzgerald

Jeremy Sherman

Contents

Introduction:
Whirring at Night

Indecision is no big deal when life is going well enough, which for many of us is most of the time. But sometimes late at night when everyone else has been sleeping for hours, your darkened bedroom expands to encompass a vast swirl of alternatives, many writ large and terrible.

Trapped in doubt, you can't find the switch that turns thought off until morning. Bouncing off each other's provocations, your mind, heart, and body jolt you with anxious ticks and questions, visions of choosing wrong, or having already chosen wrong and suffering the humiliating consequences. Indecision is an awful thing. No wonder we are at such pains to avoid it.

The indecision that first got me wondering about uncertainty was wondering whether my son was crazy or I was an awful parent. By day he would amaze my wife and me with extraordinary acts of cluelessness. By night I'd struggle to interpret. *Will he ever come round*, I wondered as the glowing minute hand went its relentless rounds. *Is his belligerence a phase, a screw loose, or an indictment of me? What should I do? What can I expect if I continue to do what I'm doing, if I continue to fall short of what I should be?*

Practice breeds familiarity. After many sleep-deprived years I came to know the contours of this one uncertainty. By the time my son was a teen, I had tried everything but consistency. I had ping-ponged all over the table until I could see two simple sides clearly. One, I called *Lazy*; the other, *Limited*.

Lazy meant my son just wasn't trying hard enough. He could get off drugs and stop hating and sabotaging, but instead he was having indulgent fun at everyone's expense. It had to stop. I had to stop it, and why wasn't I holding him to a reasonable standard, and what could I expect for being a lax parent but this disaster?

Limited meant that he couldn't help his behavior. It was, as several doctors told us, a psycho-physical limitation—a neuroanatomical impairment as straightforward as Down's syndrome, even though it didn't seem like it. By expecting what he could not supply, I was only damaging him more. Where was my heart? Why was I so angry at him? What kind of father feels shame and rage at his son's biological limitations?

My father interpreted my son's behavior as an indulgence, and always attentive to his commanding voice, I heard him well when he urged me to take command. Then my father got very sick with cancer and I watched him deal with his own different sleep-depriving doubt.

The story goes that in the early morning after his diagnosis, lying awake with my mother, my father farted.

"Cured," he said.

If it were that simple, he could then roll over and fall asleep. The tough call that kept him up throughout his surviving years was whether it was better to accept or resist his declining health. As the cancer progressed he wondered incessantly whether he was dying because he wasn't trying hard enough, or trying so hard because he was kidding himself. Is it better to persist or let go? The Quakers have a saying that captures it: "Build to last 100 years, be ready to leave tomorrow." It's hard to do both at once.

My mother attended to him and tried to assuage his indecision. Then when he died she spent a full year mourning, wondering if she had done right by him. Had she cared for him attentively enough? If so, why did he die at 59? Then she discovered her own cancer—lung metastasized to the brain. Again I watched a loved one torn between persisting and letting go. She too died at 59.

Shortly after her death, indecision took up residence in my marriage. My wife and I spent three years negotiating by day and wondering by night: First, *How can we save this marriage?* Then, *Can we save this marriage?* And then, as divorcing individuals, *If this is what blind-faith commitment gets us, what is it good for anyway?*

I had also been working for close to a year on a new product that I thought was a no-brainer. I had invested a lot in R&D which had revealed that its path to market was quite cobbled with problems Should I persist or let go? The same dilemmas followed me wherever I went.

Tao-winism: Don't Panic, It's Organic

During this, my great mid-life season of doubt, I took some comfort from Buddhist and Taoist philosophy, which encourages us to relax into uncertainty and savor the great mysteries of life. But its calming words were never enough. I knew I shouldn't sweat it, but I sweated it anyway. I wanted to accept life as is, but in striving to do so I was trying to improve it. While many advocates of Eastern philosophy that I was listening to at this time suggested ways to resolve accepting and not accepting into one harmonious state, I noticed that ancient writers let the ambiguity stand. "Tao" translates as The Way, meaning either the way things are which you should accept, or the way to be with how things are which you should strive for. They didn't explain how the Tao could be all-encompassing and yet you could be in it or not. They didn't reconcile the tension between lines like "The Tao gives birth to both good and evil." "If you want to accord with the Tao, just do your job, then let go."

I found more comfort when I discovered an explanation for my sweatiness in Darwinism. Reading the vast and growing literature in life science for the layperson, I recognized that if you want an up-to-date sense of the Tao, you couldn't do much better than evolutionary theory, the most rigorous assessment so far of what life force really is, not its origins perhaps, but how it had played out through billions of years. This is not as long as the 11 billion years that the universe is said to exist, but the life sciences are so much closer to home than the quarks and string theories. It seemed more modest to extrapolate from life's processes to mine rather than making the quantum leap into physics.

The combination of Taoism and Darwinism—Taowinism, I called it—was a more satisfying system than Taoism alone because it both encouraged me to relax and enabled me to forgive myself when I couldn't. I did a kind of *find/replace* operation on the 2500-year-old Tao-te-ching, thinking "evolution," wherever the word Tao appeared and was delighted to find such high resonance in what resulted:

"When you realized where you come from
you naturally become tolerant, disinterested, amused
kindhearted as a grandmother, dignified as a king.
Immersed in the wonders of [Evolution]
you can deal with whatever life brings you
and when death comes, you are ready.

I realized that while I was dedicated to the pursuit of happiness, the evolutionary process—a Tao that I'm sure would have amazed and delighted the ancient masters—wasn't out to make us happy or sad, or anything other than functional in addressing certain kinds of recurring dilemmas, and this got me more interested in the kinds of dilemmas that recur.

I found more comfort and, by now, true satisfaction when I mixed Taowinism with a number of academic disciplines that shine light on the recurring dilemmas and life's extraordinary ever-evolving capacities to address them: decision theory, systems theory, complexity, behavioral economics, statistics, social psychology, and epistemology. Filling in details about how life handles tough judgment calls, they provide a sort of field guide to the common dance moves we creatures make in dealing with dilemmas. By this time I was having so much fun glimpsing the meaning of life through the life and social sciences that I went and got a Ph.D.

I took such comfort in discovering that I was not alone in my doubts that I fell into this research into the parallels between the tough judgment calls in my life and in all of life. Call it *Hmmmology*—the study of things that make you go "Hmmm . .." in the night.

In biology, a homology is a true parallel—for example, the parallel between dog's hind legs and your legs, both of which were inherited from common ancestors. Hmmmology is a search for true parallels between the problems that cause you to lie awake at night wondering what to do, and the kinds of problems that have stumped others—other humans but also other living things.

We'll call these parallel problems that life has been wondering about the "Wonderings of the World." They are the universal tough judgment calls, and let's say they come in sevens.

11

Introduction

Let's say that there are Seven Wonderings of the Ancient World—conundrums that have challenged life for its entire 3.5 billion year career on earth—and Seven Wonderings of the Modern World—conundrums that have singled out us humans ever since we gained our unique cognitive powers. If we could distill all of life's uncertainties down to these fourteen generic dilemmas, what would they be? Obviously there are many ways one could categorize the world's dilemmas. What follows then is not a definitive list, but rather, my first crack at it, having spent the last decade's studying them.

Seven Wonderings of the Ancient World

Whether or not God made the universe in seven days, life emerged with seven types of dilemmas that have kept it wondering ever since: the seven wonderings of the ancient world—life's original tough judgment calls, over three and a half billion years old and still causing us to wonder what to do. Here's a first pass at them, including forms they might take in your everyday life.

1. Should I join this? (Join vs. Don't Join)

"Can I trust him?"

"Will this pay off?"

2. Should I stick with this? (Hold vs. Fold)

"Is it time to bail?"

"Is this ever going to get better?"

3. Should I be consistent here? (Consistency vs. Flexibility)

"Maybe I'm being wishy-washy."

"Why am I so inflexible?"

4. Can I improve this? (Accept vs. Exert)

"Maybe I just have to accept."

"Why am I taking this lying down?"

5. Is this a cue? (Attend vs. Ignore)

"Why do I care what he thinks?"

"What did she mean by that?"

6. How do I move this? (Push vs. Pull)

"Should I have been kinder?"

"Is it time to get tough?"

7. Is There a Win/Win Solution? (Win/lose vs. Win/win)

"People have tried it already, what am I doing trying again?"

"There must be a better way."

The Seven Wonderings of the Modern World

We humans live in two worlds—the real one that all living things occupy and a newfangled one inside our heads in which we can imagine far more and far different things than are before our eyes. This mind's eye is the source of great new guidance for dealing with the seven wonderings of the ancient world, but is also the source of some new, distinctly human conundrums—the seven wonderings of the modern world:

1. How long should I wait? (Short-term vs. Long-term)

"I can't stand how fat I've gotten. Why can't I control myself?"

"I would be so much happier if I quit school and took a simple job."

2. Is something amiss? (Change Plans vs. Change Expectations)

"It's not what I had in mind. Should I go for it anyway?"

"Why do I keep putting off my priorities?"

3. Can this person change? (Limited vs. Lazy)

"Is this kid lazy or handicapped?"

"He says he'll stop drinking but he doesn't. Should I believe him?"

4. Should I look at this? (Address vs. Don't)

"Maybe I should just get over it."

"Maybe we should confront her and talk it out, but would it help?"

5. Should I be more realistic? (Dream vs. Reality)

"This is the wake-up call. Why have I been so unrealistic?"

"Why is this company is so stodgy and uncreative?"

6. Should I say it? (Truth vs. Care)

"She asked for my feedback, so why is she so upset?"

"Why didn't he tell me he thought I was making a mistake?"

7. How Should I know myself? (Conviction vs. Doubt)

"Why am I always second-guessing myself?"

"Why was I in denial so long?"

Will Wonders Never Cease?

A sense of wonder is a wonderful thing, but the wonder that stalks you in bed is not. You don't invite it. You turn a corner and find it there. It's a good thing that for most of us it comes rarely and stays briefly. It is not welcome.

One common element of most, if not all, doubt is our reaction to it: Most people, when in doubt, imagine a happy state beyond all doubt, a place one could go where wonders cease.

Asked how we're doing on a bad day, we are likely to allude to this wonder-free place, either as where we'll be once we solve some current conundrum or as a place that more skillful or fortunate souls occupy—your heroes, movie stars and millionaires, tribal people from long ago, contented gurus from other lands, fictional characters, the writers of self-help and business books, and the successful people they report upon who follow their advice religiously.

Few of us would explicitly defend a belief in the possibility of doubt-free existence, but in subtle ways most of us harbor a dream of ultimately finding a doubt-free zone.

Surely one reason so many of us love to immerse ourselves in a good movie or a long book is that, for a spell, we enjoy an existence free from forks in the mental road—nothing to decide, the path stretching on ahead for miles, clearly marked, with no alternative routes to make you wonder if you are on the right path. It's like riding an express train to get to the destination at the end of the line. Your decision-making mind can afford to fall asleep. You don't have to worry about missing your stop, waking up and wondering if you are in the right place or have already passed the fork where you were supposed part company with the train.

In contrast, think of the relatively trivial panhandler's question, "Can you spare a quarter?" If you have a clear and certain policy that you won't ever give money to panhandlers, then the path is clear. But if you are the kind of person who sometimes gives, then the path is forked. Does this panhandler deserve your money? Will it go toward self-improvement or wine? Are you gullible for giving the quarter or callous for not? It won't kill you to lose a quarter. It's not the quarter that makes the encounter taxing; it's the doubt.

15

Introduction

Confidence feels so good. Doubt feels so bad. The dream of a doubt-free existence is well fed by anyone marketing a service, a theory, a religion, or a self-help practice implying a surefire solution.

If doubt were a rare affliction for which an effective vaccine existed or a disease like chicken pox that once contracted never recurs, then the study of doubt would hardly be worth our time. But a persistently doubt-free place is a figment. Doubt can't be eradicated like smallpox. Wonders don't cease. Completing one mid-life crisis, we do well to recognize that if we're lucky to live long enough there will be more. There is no "I once was lost but now I'm found" worth counting on.

Doubt is only getting more recurrent and unavoidable, increasing at an unprecedented rate. To list just a few reasons, people today face more choices about how to live than ever before, and every choice means more doubt about the choices you've made. Many of the new choices are untested, so we can't know whether they will pay off. Melting pot culture means working and dwelling in more mixed company than people used to, and their contrasting beliefs and choices pose an ever-present challenge that erodes the resolve we accumulate in support of the choices we have made. Unlike those in the past who believed that the rewards for their choices would assuredly come in the afterlife, we hope to get the results of our choices within our lifetimes. We know that the choices we make will make or break us in no time. We hear more stories about people whose choices turned out bad, people who would have been better served by doubting more. Our expectations are higher too. We have the self-made man and woman,—fabulous rags to riches stories that tempt us to choose well so we too could be so lucky.

Recent history is littered with evidence for the benefit of doubt. We cultivate a cultural of skepticism, born of the last few centuries' phenomenally successful and unprecedented questioning of authority and tradition. Schools promote critical thinking—the habit of doubt—and taken to its logical conclusion, doubt has become a lifestyle choice itself for orthodox skeptics, post-modern philosophy buffs, and, above all, the lovers of irony, any fan of modern comedy with its delicious and consoling emphasis on parody of the staid and stodgy. The age of doubt has arrived, and you are here in the thick of it.

With no surefire way to prevent infection and reinfection, doubt is worth our attention. We do well to wonder what it is, where it comes from, what different doubts have in common, whether doubt is useful and if so when, and why and if it's useful does it hurt so much?

These questions might stir a curious mind, always on the lookout for a little intellectual stimulation, but even for those of us who get enough stimulation, there are very practical reasons to study doubt. When you know the nature of doubt, you dance with your doubts more skillfully. It helps you make better decisions and live more comfortably with the decisions you make.

Before proceeding though, I'd like to let you know that I'm about to cut out, writing the rest of this book as though it were about you and us rather than me. Lest my reliance on the pronoun "you," seem too imposing, I'd like to confess that by "you," I mostly mean "me." Writing pop management and psychology books is in large part a therapeutic exercise for us authors. It can be one of the most effective things you can do to reinforce your self-development practice. A cigarette smoker can motivate herself to quit by formally announcing to her friends that she is going to do so. On a grander scale, attaching your name to a published prescription is very motivational. A diet book author has more reason to stick with his or her diet than any of the book's readers. This is one reason why there are so many books of this kind. The saying goes, "Those who can't do, teach," but those who are still working on doing teach too, learning by chanting over and over to the crowds they can gather whatever it is that they need to learn. At our best, we authors are writing to ourselves, like talking to ourselves out loud. The "you" that you see throughout the remainder of this book may or may not ring true to who you are, but it does ring true to me. By writing this book, I'm negotiating with myself. Authors of books like this are notorious for exempting themselves from their own advice since they are already experts in it. Every bit of advice in this book is advice I must repeatedly give myself. The slogan and titles for each helpful hint were things I coined or heard that served as shorthand mantras to help me put and keep my doubts in order. So please take my "you," in the self-inclusive sense with which I intend it.

Take It Personally (T.I.P.)

Darn, I've wasted most of my life learning things I now already know.

Even before looking at doubt, get good at spotting the illusion that you could ever get beyond it to a place where you never made a wrong move, where there are no bets—only sure things.

Next time you are in a bookstore, scan the shelves for books that promise once-and-for-all solutions. There are many.

Next time you find yourself in a conversation that's moving a little slowly, use your spare attention to listen for allusions to the doubt-free zone.

Remember times in your past when friends came to you very excited about having found some important and broad truth? Was their elation driven by a sense of relief—that now, guided by their new truth, they would be forever freed from doubt about something that used to eat at them regularly? In your own past, do you remember ever feeling this kind of elation?

It is possible to find important truths that reduce doubt significantly for whole stretches. The point here is not that all "surefire" solutions are useless, but simply to notice our appetite for them. We love finding what feels like a surefire way to make our path forward more clear. Tough judgment calls make us balk.

Of course, not all of them. Life without challenge is boring. There's nothing as thrilling as a tough call that tests and proves how smart we're getting. The doubts we can reason our way through are fun precisely because of the prevalence of doubts that we can't reason our way through. Proving our prowess with almost overwhelming doubts affirms our accumulated mastery.

Benefits of the Doubt

There are five high-pay-off practical benefits to cultivating doubt management skills.

1. Lonely no more: Stop assuming that the fact that you still doubt means there's something wrong with you. Why you? Why anybody and everybody?

2. Less time on useless doubt: Not asking "why me?" saves time and makes you smarter. Knowing that residual doubt is inevitable saves time spent rehashing done deals.

3. Less shirking of healthy doubt: Inoculate yourself with ample antidotes to the spellbinding allure of certainty. Knowing how doubt works closes off the escape hatches that keep us from making good use of doubt worth heeding.

4. Better analogies: In unfamiliar circumstances, we look to parallels in the familiar to guide our decisions. Bad parallels = bad choices. When you familiarize yourself with the fundamental forms that doubt takes, they become your best analogies.

5. From doubt to wonder: When you appreciate life's venerable legacy of dealing with tough judgment calls, you feel at home, ready to take your turn, and tooled-up with a reliable meaning of life and a sense of how wonderful it is.

Benefit 1: Lonely No More

Every conundrum that has ever eaten at your insides, giving you a queasy stomach, a gnawing chest, a sleepless night, or a nasty headache—every hounding thought that you have shared with loved ones until they're sick of it or suppressed so that they're spared the sickness but you aren't—appears to you as a unique challenge.

The friend who consoles with "Oh, that's just like what my friend Bert went through . . ." is off-topic, maybe slightly consoling, but missing the point. You aren't Bert and your friend's not paying attention. Your details are different.

When in doubt, in addition to asking, "What should I do?" people automatically ask, "Why me? Other people know what to do. What explains my unique lack of clarity?"

There are only a few possible answers. One, you're dumber than everyone else. Two, there's a conspiracy out there messing with your mind exclusively. Three, something exceptional happened in your childhood that made you unusually bent.

Now a therapist won't endorse the first two. But if your problems aren't somewhat exceptional then what would justify your requirement for therapy? The third reason does: Go fishing around in your past and you're bound to find the source of your exceptional bentness.

Indeed, your past will go a long way toward explaining your particular bent. Still, never underestimate the pervasiveness of doubt. The most profound answer to "Why you?" is "Why anyone and everyone?"

Luck hasn't singled you out as the one to harass. Everyone is thumping on the same conundrums. The kind of problems that keep you up at night don't matter just in your life, not even just in all human life, but in all of life, from bacterium to a brainiac like you.

Life has been sweating tough decisions for a very long time and doing a brilliant job of it too. Life is not stumped by these conundrums. It's working on them. Adapting and evolving, it's been patiently collecting the tools that help us make a phenomenal amount of tough calls pretty well—mostly right answers. When it comes to tough calls you are a reigning master. Over the millennia, wise guidance for making tough judgment calls stuck to your family tree like flies to sap. For most of these three and a half billion years, they accumulated as biological adaptations—molecular configurations, genomes, organs, traits, instincts, behaviors— all embodied wisdom and all for dealing with universal dilemmas that manifest in myriad ways.

With the right tools for the job, your family made millions of right choices in dealing with tough judgment calls, which is why you're here at all, connected in an uninterrupted line to your first microbial ancestor billions of years ago. You've got quite the toolkit for dealing with the wonders already.

Stop to appreciate the simple fact that in billions of years, not one member of your family line faltered, failing to pass on a toolkit before death. The longest marathon ever, and truly lucky you arriving here—not at the finish line for there isn't one, but arriving nonetheless at this moment when so many other creatures didn't for lack of sufficiently wise guidance. You're a tournament champ—not like the billions of would-have-been offspring of now-extinct species and extinguished family lines.

Next, appreciate your general lack of appreciation: One of the great tools you inherited was your capacity to ignore the tools that work. That way you can concentrate instead on a wonder's current, brain-teasing manifestations.

You can't possibly attend to all judgment calls. So when a tool works reliably, you think about something else, most likely a squeakier wheel. This selective obliviousness is very efficient. Without it you might never get a good night's sleep.

The discomfort you feel when listening to a squeaky wheel is a useful tool also. Like an alarm clock, it wakes you up to an opportunity to choose that you might not want to miss. Doubt is functionally uncomfortable because it forces you to take active steps to address a dilemma, but since the discomfort is uncomfortable, it also makes us wish the tough judgment calls would just go away.

Take It Personally (T.I.P.)

It comes with the territory.

Doubt is a necessary evil, but self-doubt about doubt—disappointment with yourself for feeling doubt—is usually unnecessary and reduces your chances of making good decisions.

Next time you stumble into the kind of indecision that makes you feel inadequate, distract yourself from the "Why me?" question by remembering that doubt comes with territory. Don't think about the poor sap whom your friend wants you to know is like you. Think about us all and how doubt is not your special flaw. We all have it, and the more interesting and exciting you make your life; the better you have got to be at digesting it.

Benefit 2: Less Time on Useless Doubt

The second payoff for coming to terms with doubt is less time spent on doubt.

Some of this increased efficiency results from asking one question instead of two. Instead of asking both "What should I do?" and "Why me?" you need only ask "What should I do?" This will save you not only the time you used to spend on "Why me?" but more than that because self-doubt makes it harder to think straight. Doubt and self-doubt create a vicious cycle that dissolves when you reduce self-doubt. Breaking the cycle should cut time spent in doubt significantly, but the benefits are even greater than that.

Even more, coming to terms with doubt also reduces second-guessing by decoupling the persistence of doubt from the impulse to reopen decisions. Here's how.

When you make a decision you expect immediate relief. After all, you have taken action. There should be something to show for it. There are two reasons why, to our surprise and disappointment, we get little relief after making a decision. They have to do with the two fundamental features of tough judgment calls.

First, a tough judgment call is a choice among alternative bets, not certainties. If they weren't bets, it wouldn't be tough. You've made a bet. You expect relief but all you get is a commitment to a speculation. No wonder it's unsettling.

Second, by definition, a tough judgment call is a choice between alternative mixed bags, each of which has a combination of costs and benefits. When you've made a choice, you instantly find yourself strapped with newly assumed costs—the ones that accompany the choice you've made—and giving up benefits you would have enjoyed with any options you didn't take. You are likely therefore to think something is amiss, as though you shouldn't have chosen yet or you chose wrong. So you're tempted to move back into decision-making mode.

Coming to terms with the fundamental features of doubt— that everyone does it, that it doesn't go away when you make a choice, and that choosing puts you in immediate touch with disappointment over costs you've accepted and benefits you've forgone—reduces the tendency to reopen decisions. It removes the tendency to be a decision-making wallflower who won't decide or a decision-making wall-bouncer, who ping-pongs between options, bouncing from wall to wall with infinite second-guessing. This will save you lots of time.

Take It Personally (T.I.P.)

Are you expressing a feeling or reopening a decision?

You've made a decision, and now you feel bad. You're talking to a friend about the good things you gave up and the bad things you took on by choosing a certain option. Pretty soon, you're rethinking the decision as if you haven't made it yet.

Feeling bad after making a decision is not necessarily a reason to remake your decision. Sometimes it's useful to revisit decisions, but you wouldn't want to do it automatically, translating "Ouch" into "Uh oh" and going from "Uh oh" automatically to "Hmmm ..."

It's so easy to slip from declaring ambivalence into reopening a decision. And if circumstances don't permit remaking your decision, it's all too easy to channel your disappointment into anger and resentment aimed at those who won't let you change your mind. Knowing that it is easy to slip is sometimes all it takes to control these tendencies.

Benefit 3: Less Shirking of Healthy Doubt

Since being efficient about dealing with doubt frees you for more enjoyable activities, why not eliminate all doubt? Because sometimes doubt is extremely useful. A third benefit of coming to terms with doubt is that it helps you corner yourself with doubt worth having by eliminating inappropriate escape routes. After all, you're not just after a good night's sleep—you want better judgment calls when they're called for. Confronting your choicest choice points can be uncomfortable, but it is worth the trouble no matter what time of day or night. And the better you get at confronting your decisions by day, the less they'll stack up over your head during the graveyard shift.

A doubt is a fork in the road. All it takes to turn a fork into a straightaway is blocking off one of the branches. Don't risk stalling out with indecision, just blow right through the intersection. We do this all the time and usually quite appropriately. Think of the thousands of decisions you make automatically. At this very moment you have the option to run naked in the streets, but you ignore it. The choice doesn't even come to mind. You fork-edit.

Your embodied wisdom—all the adaptations you inherited from your ancestors and the learning gleaned in the course of your life—can be thought of as a collection of rules for fork-editing, enabling you to both ignore decisions that can make themselves and to make good decisions at the inescapable forks that consume your attention until you make a decision.

But in the gray area between the obviously ignorable forks and the forks that you definitely have to address lie all the forks that may or may not be worth attending to. With these you have to decide whether to decide.

Weighing in favor of fork-editing so you don't have to make an active decision is the discomfort you feel when in doubt. Since it's no fun to be in doubt you've naturally accumulate a few bits of false guidance that feel good because they enable you to avoid the discomfort of doubt, even when it would be better to face it. They are ways of saying "Just fork-edit," even when in the long run it's going to cost you. We typically prune forking branches with shorthand words or phrases that imply rules.

For example, in bed one night, you find yourself wondering whether you should stay in your current job or quit. You remember that your father used to say, "Persistence furthers." That sounds like answer enough. In a choice between persisting at anything or shifting to something else, always persist.

But really, sometimes persistence furthers and sometimes it doesn't. Whether sticking with your job is one of those cases where persistence furthers is precisely why you're wondering in the first place, so employing some preposterously sweeping generalization is missing the point (probably on purpose). It's a way to just fork-edit.

"Persistence furthers" is a neat two-word branch-pruner. But you can also prune that branch with a single word: "Quitter." A quitter is someone who has made a bad choice. Calling a job-leaver a quitter automatically implies a sweeping rule that leaving is always the wrong choice. Should you leave? No way are you a quitter, so just fork-edit. Don't quit. Now go back to sleep.

But before you nod off, notice that you could just as easily prune the other branch with a single word. People who stay in a job too long are sheep, mindlessly complying with expectations. Being a sheep is baaaad. Equate staying in your job with sheepishness instead of quitting, and it becomes instantly obvious that you should quit your job. Having let a different unexamined rule (never be sheepish) make your decision for you, you can now go back to sleep.

Einstein said that a theory should be as simple as possible but no simpler. We all need rules of thumb to help us with decision making, but rules like "persistence furthers, don't be a quitter" or "don't be a sheep" are simply too simple.

F. Scott Fitzgerald said, "The test of first-rate intelligence is the ability to hold two opposed ideas in the mind at the same time and still be able to function." If it's absolutely bad to be a quitter and it's also absolutely bad to be a sheep, it goes to show that these sweeping generalizations can't really make your decision for you after all. Being sweeping, they can make you feel decisive, but feeling decisive and making good decisions are two different things.

With each of the wonderings of the ancient world and of the modern world, therefore, we'll list a few of the dangerous terms and phases commonly used to disguise tough calls as no-brainers. We'll call these false rules *Just fork-edits*.

Coming to terms with doubt means familiarizing yourself with commonly used Just fork-edits. To name them is to tame them. They won't be as effective for glossing over important decisions and that's a good thing.

Take it Personally (T.I.P.)
Every maxim is a half-truth. To find the other half, ask yourself why, if it's so true, do people need to say it?

If persistence really always furthers, why bother saying it? After all, anything that is consistently true and obvious should go without saying.

A simple explanation for repeating the obvious is that people are simply too thickheaded to do the right thing without reminders of what it is. This explanation has some appeal, especially if one delivers it with the air of detached amusement about the thickness of other people, but really, why would a creature with our track record for flexible adaptation and learning consistently do the wrong thing? Often for some overlooked advantage it confers that makes it part-right.

Next time you hear a broad attractive truth, rather than merely nodding your head in affirmation, take a moment to ask yourself why, if it engenders so much head nodding consent, it doesn't simply go without saying. Then think of what it's up against, and not just some groundless thickheaded resistance, but rather some well-founded half-truth—the other side of the same coin.

Benefit 4: Better Analogies

We humans are the only living creatures that can do significant amounts of reasoning by analogy. To us, everything is at least a little bit like something else. Dropped into unfamiliar territory you'll first say, "Gee, this is unfamiliar," and then immediately set to work figuring out what features of it are like features of other situations you've been in before. This makes you extremely flexible, able to make good choices in dealing with the unfamiliar.

A toaster is like an oven in that it heats food, like a mailbox in that it has a slot, like a bread box in that it holds baked goods on the kitchen counter, like a water heater in that it has an electrical element, like a car in that it has chrome plating . . . the list goes on, but most of the time we don't keep adding to it. Consciousness is a pinhole in a flood. We can't afford to think of all possible analogies so we usually make do with the first ones to come to mind. Those first analogies determine a lot about how we relate to the unfamiliar.

Up at night, stumped and wondering if you should change jobs, you don't know what to do because the situation feels unfamiliar. Then you remember that your Dad always used to say, "It's always darkest before the dawn." You should therefore persist because your job is like the darkness. It is about to get brighter.

But really, is your job's chance of improving like the sun's chance of rising? While it may be darkest before dawn, it's also darkest before death. Perhaps your Mom always used to say, "Don't flog a dead horse," and the dead horse, not the dawn, is what comes to mind first. You should quit.

Who is right, Mom or Dad? One satisfying but specious analogy may help you get a good night's sleep, but you wouldn't want it to make your decisions for you. Two opposing analogies could be useful, but mostly in looping you back around to the question you started with.

It matters, therefore, how you pick your analogies. Pick the wrong ones and you'll make the wrong decisions. Digging into doubt, including how we use analogies to end it, provides you with a better fitting set of analogies to draw upon.

Knowing the wonderings of the ancient and modern worlds is like owning a field guide that helps you identify the things that fly by in your life. It helps you make better decisions; it familiarizes you with the basic patterns of human and natural affairs so that you can work with them most efficiently and productively.

Take it Personally (T.I.P.)

Nothing is Just Anything.

Notice the analogies you draw. Make them more explicit rather than letting them work on your unconscious. When someone says a certain task must be accomplished by a team, not an individual, because "You can't make honey from one bee," stop to think about the extent to which the task is like making honey and that an individual is like a bee. Put your parallels on the table in front of you where you can keep an eye on them.

A word to keep an especially attentive eye on is "just," as in "My job is just like the dawn." If your job is just like the dawn, then it is not like anything else, and you should stick with it because like the dawn, it will break into lightness soon. Just is used to end Wonder— to terminate the search for analogies. Nothing enables us to just fork-edit like that little word just, so notice when it comes up. And when it does, remind yourself that nothing is just anything.

Benefit 5: From Doubt to Wonder

One final reason to study doubt: Not only does it translate into better decision-making and more peace of mind, but it is as direct a route as you'll ever find for getting into to the more wonderful kind of wonder. Your doubt is a strand you can follow into as rich a version of the meaning of life as you'll ever need or find.

Life has had to make tough judgment calls all along. It's been a fork-finding mission from the get-go. Think how many forks there are: the forking branches of the great tree of life, of family trees, of every choice you make; the forks that branch from few to many, your options at this moment, for example, or the outgrowth from an original ancestral species into many and varied species; the forks from many to few — your past decisions which narrowed your options or the tree of death from many original ancestral lineages to the surviving lineages today. What do all these forks have in common?

Something about the selective process moves life along the branches. The craving for wisdom for dealing with life's forks is life force itself. Described this way, it's not some lofty or esoteric thing. Decisions press and we don't want to blow it. We don't want to be fooled again or waste years barking up the wrong tree. We humans feel pleasure when we find wisdom and pain when our wisdom falls short.

What we have in common with bacteria is not that we want the same things, but rather that we share some of the same dilemmas. The wonderings of the ancient world that bacteria faced continue to keep you wondering. Recognizing this won't make you want to live as one in harmony with all bacteria, but it will make the world seem a more harmonious place, with all of us working on parallel challenges.

This living appetite for the wisdom by which to make better choices is fundamental to simple human pleasures. To bring it home, football fascinates many people, and those whom it doesn't fascinate are fascinated by the fact that it fascinates others. Football championships involve forks too. You've seen the branching diagrams, many teams at the branch tips who through successive trial-and-error sifting filter down to a single champion team.

You acquired your decision-making wisdom by a trial-and-error sifting too. In your ancestry and within your life, both nature and nurture have in common this trial-and-error sifting for useful tools that enable you to make good decisions.

In biology this sifting process is most commonly known as survival of the fittest, though the phrase is misleading for two reasons. First, it's not really survival of the fittest, but rather survival of the fit-enough. Unlike a football championship that ends with one team supreme, life's sifting is more accommodating. A body doesn't have to reign supreme. It just has to get through the sifter. Second, it's not survival of the physically fit, but rather survival of those creatures who fit their circumstances like a hand in a fine glove.

What selects? In biology, nature does;_as in Darwin's *natural* selection—Fit is what The Wisdom is all about. All living beings need to make decisions that fit the opportunities and circumstances presented to them. All adaptations—whether physical, behavioral, emotional, or mental—are wisdom that contributes to making a good fit between a creature and its circumstances.

We humans aren't equipped at birth with all of the instinctual wisdom we need in order to solve all the problems we will encounter in our lives. To glean the wisdom we need, we have a natural curiosity about the ways of the world. Learning from broad experience is pretty mushy, since we can't often tell what causes what. Our curiosity is well served with human-scale simulations of the bigger world we live in. Games, with their simple, definite rules, their beginnings, middles and ends, are great this way, but so are crafts, stories, and anything else that shrinks and concretizes cause and effect at a level at which we can appreciate it and then apply it metaphorically to other situations we encounter. Enjoying a football championship is a good way to gain a visceral sense of life's sifting processes. Football, quilting, jazz improvisation—they all teach life lessons we can apply to business, and life in general.

Indeed all sports, hobbies, and arts—all opportunities to pursue or experience mastery—provide us a way to savor what could be called *Pattern Sensuality*, a chance to savor the contours of general patterns that show up everywhere. These endeavors are luscious fun at the small scale of their details and particulars. They are enjoyable in part because they aren't played on a grand scale. When the game or quilt or story is done you don't have to think about it anymore. But they are also pleasurable because you can't help but carry forward the wisdom you glean in them—wisdom for dealing with the doubts or wonderings of the world.

Stepping back to appreciate the fundamental interplay of doubt and the wisdom for dealing with it enhances hobbies and can become a hobby in itself. You are lucky to be alive now when scientists are solving so many mysteries about the how life solves dilemmas. At the end of the book you'll find a short natural history of doubt and wisdom (in four acts) and a list of great sources for more information.

Take it Personally (T.I.P.)
To sweat the petty less, pet the sweaty more.

Wishing that doubt would go away, you might sometimes try to convince yourself that you should just stop all your wondering and relax. This Don't-sweat-the-small-stuff approach may be a comfort, but it's a very short-lived one. Yes, some stuff really does turn out to be small stuff, and no, you don't want to waste time sweating it. But some stuff is scary as hell and the fact that from 50,000 feet up with a wide-angle lens the big stuff looks small won't help much because you don't live out there. You live here, at the scale where bad things happen and they hurt a lot.

Coming to terms with doubt is like making friends with a formidable beast—petting the doubts that make you sweat. This action will help you differentiate between things worth sweating and things not worth sweating. It will enable you to sweat less of the really small stuff.

Whatever you get for the bets you place in life, one thing you are sure to get for petting the sweaty is the satisfaction of finding out something more about why you are here and what all the sweat is about. People miss this who try to convince themselves that it's all no sweat.

Indecision-atomy

The doubts that eat at us generally have a few common features.

Rising to conscious awareness: Choosing entails paring down options until you have an obvious action to take. Most paring down happens automatically, so most choosing happens automatically too, when your gut has eliminated all but one option. Choices become active when the paring down is incomplete.

You can picture easy judgment calls as a process whereby options are weeded out unconsciously and the select few sift their way single file through a narrow portal into action like football champs striding triumphant on the field of play. But when two or more options arrive at the portal simultaneously, they jam. Deciding what to do becomes a matter your conscious awareness to sort out.

Two options: We are masterful at paring down options. Most don't even get consciously considered. Therefore the door-jamming choices are likely to have been pared down to the minimum, which is two. Of course a doubt may come to you as a choice among more than two options. That's because you can face multiple doubts at once. Even the most complex dilemmas get simplified down to two options or a continuum between two poles.

High stakes: Choosing right feels important, either because the short- or long-term costs of getting it wrong are high or because you don't get to change your mind later without it costing a lot.

Ambiguous cues: Each of your two options could turn out to be the right choice under different conditions or by different standards; you just can't get a good read on which conditions or standards apply.

Divergent solutions: Each option in the pair suggests opposite actions making it difficult or impossible to take both actions at once.

It was Ben Franklin who gave us the tried and true method for dealing with tough judgment calls. You fold a sheet of paper into quarters, using the left side to represent one option and the right side to represent the other. The top quadrants are the upsides—the reasons in favor of an option—and the bottom quadrants are the downsides—the reasons against an option. Tough decisions are those in which something of substance appears in each quarter—good reasons for and against both options.

Consider a simple choice between two solutions to a dilemma that's causing you doubt, Plan A and Plan B, in which you have two cues X and Y that will tip you off as to which plan is the right solution:

If (X) then (Plan A).

If (Y) then (Plan B).

Suppose again that you are trying to decide whether to leave your job or stick with it:

If (dead-end) then (leave)..

If (growth opportunity) then (stay).

When it's easy to tell whether the job is a dead-end or a growth opportunity, it's easy to know what to do. Even if you couldn't tell whether it were a dead-end or a growth opportunity, if it were easy to both leave and stay then the decision would still be a snap.

The decisions that cause us acid indigestion are the ones in which it is very hard to tell whether the situation is X or Y, and you can't easily hedge by doing Plan A and B at the same time. It is very difficult to simultaneously quit and stay at a job, so if you are having a difficult time deciding whether it is a dead-end or a growth opportunity, you'll have a doubt eating at you. Call these tough ones *A.C.I.D.S.*, which stands for *Ambiguous Cues Implying Divergent Solutions.*

Picture yourself trying to climb to higher job satisfaction. If you get clear and obvious clues that your job is a growth opportunity, then you should stay, which in the first illustration is like heading to the right. Likewise if you know that the job is a dead end, then you should leave, which in the second illustration is like heading to the left.

Likewise if you know that the job is a dead end, then you should leave, which below is like heading to the left.

"Ambiguous cues" translate as an inability to determine on which hillside you really stand. Heading to the right makes great sense if it's a growth opportunity, but if it's a dead-end, heading right will only lower your job satisfaction. Likewise, heading to the left makes great sense if it's a dead-end, but if you are really situated on a growth opportunity, leaving means a decline in satisfaction, not an increase. If your cues are ambiguous, you face upsides and downsides in each direction.

And actually, the "A" in A.C.I.D.S. could also stand for "ambivalent." Whereas *ambiguous* cues are conditions in the outside world that are hard to read, *ambivalent* cues are conditions within yourself that are hard to read. You are of two minds, wanting two different things at once that are to some extent mutually exclusive.

Imagine that you are considering whether to continue to work as a free-lancer or take a salaried position somewhere. You value both the freedom you have as a free-lancer and the security you would have in a salaried position. Reading your own heart, you find multiple motives and you can't make up your mind. You feel ambivalence.

If you concentrate on your appetite for freedom, then freelancing is the clear and certain way to go. If instead you concentrate on your appetite for security, then getting a salaried job is the way to go. Recognizing both needs, you feel ambivalence. You might compromise, getting as much freedom and security as you can, say from part-time salaried work and part-time freelancing. But how to get more? The heart strains to increase freedom by doing more freelance work but at the expense of the security you get from salaried work, and visa versa.

On a good day, part salaried and part freelancing, you might appreciate that you have managed to get a nice bit of freedom and security happening in your life. On a bad day you might look up in either or both direction and see all the freedom or security you're missing out on and wish you weren't.

This freelance vs. salaried ambivalence is a classic by the way and, as such, is a golden opportunity to illustrate how universal a dilemma can be. Should you affiliate or not? It's the first wondering of the ancient world. By affiliating with a company that can pay you a salary you get integrated into the system, gaining reliable resources but losing freedom. Translate that to your love life. With marriage you get reliable security, comfort, love, and attention, but at a sacrifice of some freedom. Freelance in love, you maintain your independence but you may never know where your next love is coming from. In marriage for instance you could feel your heart tugging both for more security and more freedom. You could wish your partner loved you more and that you had more freedom.

Translate it to politics, which is sometimes described as a fundamental irreducible tension between societal goals such as fairness or justice and individual goals such as freedom or liberty. The greater our cultural cohesion, the more constraint on freedom. The greater the freedom, the less cohesion. The counterculture didn't notice this tension when it called for both at once. "We are all one" and "If it feels good do it" can work at cross-purposes to each other, and the bind that politics wrestles with is how much all-for-one fairness to impose and how much laissez faire liberty to allow. Think of how many political debates you've heard in which two sides face off as if this tension didn't exist. One side argues, "We can't limit freedoms." The other side argues, "What matters is the good of society."

It's not all tension, of course. There are win-win situations: freelancing success that keeps you in all the work you could wish for, being with a mate who know how to have and hold with out holding too tightly, finding political solutions that achieve rich blends of both freedom and justice. As the first words of this book declare, most of the time we are not riddled with doubt. But when doubt arises, it feels as though you are facing a trade-off that appears in this A.C.I.D.S. X-like format, even if you aren't.

And so with each of the wonderings we'll do both, giving a single name to the pair of tensions involved and picturing them as a pair of hills, one of which is worth climbing, you just can't tell which.

Take it Personally (T.I.P.)

Just because you are annoyed, it doesn't mean they're annoying.

If life entails dealing with irreducible tensions such as those between identifying with the larger whole and being wholly independent, then it is perfectly possible that sometimes we will feel tense and it will be nobody's fault. The boss doesn't appreciate, let alone approve an employee's proposal, not because the boss is an annoying closed-minded dictator, but because she's forced to pay attention to the company's big picture objectives. She regards the employee as a part of the larger whole more than the employee does. The judge won't make an exception in the plaintiff's case, not because he is a control freak but because opening the system to personal exceptions costs millions more to enforce than a one-fine-fits-all approach.

Keep this in mind and you'll resist the quite natural temptation when bothered to assume that someone has done you wrong. Someone might have, and it's worth exploring, but in a world in which irreducible tension happens, making disappointment possible without anyone doing the disappointment, we're better off not automatically translating "ouch" into "how dare you?"

Sure Enough

Let's go back to bed, where we were pondering whether to continue at your current job. This time let's deliberate with a clear alternative to it. If you left, it would be to start a new business. You've got a business in mind, but you can't tell if it's going to fly.

Is your current job a dead-end, or your best option? Is this new business concept a winner or a loser? It's a tough call, so you have something in all four quadrants. Even after doing Ben Franklin's exercise in your pillowed head (because who really puts options on folded pieces of paper anyway?), neither option is a certain winner. So now what?

First, what would certainty look like anyway? With our hillsides, it would have one hill, not two. With Ben's boxes it would look either of the figures below—lots of reasons for and no reasons against one option, and no reasons for but lots of reasons against the other option. That's what a completely sure thing would look like.

	Plan A	Plan B
Pro	This and that reason Another good reason Still more good reasons Another advantage Especially good reason Furthermore	
Con		A really problem A huge disadvantage Further problems The cost that really hurts Another difficulty A big hassle

	Plan A	Plan B
Pro		This and that reason Another good reason Still more good reasons Another advantage Especially good reason Furthermore
Con	A really problem A huge disadvantage Further problems The cost that really hurts Another difficulty A big hassle	

Now, there are four ways that people deal with tough judgment calls, three of which imply holding a high standard up to this black–and-white certainty. Here they are:

Hem-haw: Don't decide. Wait for two quadrants to empty out. Say that we don't have enough information yet, stare at the options, get distracted by the inadequacy of our decision-making skills, lose sleep—anything until the pattern clears to black and white. Hem-haw has a bad reputation. It's seen as a sign of weak character.

Alternatively, we could pretend that the pattern is already black and white and we've got our certainty. There are two ways of doing this.

Ping-pong: Move with lots of confidence but no consistency. One day we're thinking the job is a dead-end and the new business is a sure thing as though the reasons for the job and against the new business don't even exist. But the next day something has perturbed our certainty and we toggle to the opposite certainty: The job is the sure thing and the business is not going to work. While you'll look indecisive to anyone who's watching, at least you don't have to examine the stuff in all four quadrants at the same time. It's like seeing a pair of oscillating mirages of certainty. Ping-ponging has a bad reputation. Like hem-haw, ping-pong is seen as disreputable and a sign of weak character.

Cocksure: Decide on one of the options, and once decided, ignore the arguments against your decision. Once you decided what to do, you simply cut out and tear up the two now-inconvenient quadrants you were considering earlier. For example, when deciding to start a new business, though there may still be arguments for the job and against the business, eradicate uncertainty by promptly forgetting these arguments. Burn up the two inconvenient quadrants and pretend that they never existed. Say that the business is going to be a surefire hit. Laugh at the people who aren't bold enough to quit their jobs. Chant the prayer, "I hope this business will succeed," but for added prayer-power, remove the words "I hope."

In the real world, cocksure is seen as a much better alternative to hem-haw or ping-pong, largely because when you're cocksure you're a known quantity, an easy read. People can tell what you stand for so they can figure out how to interact with you.

Cocksure has a great reputation, but there are costs to it. One is that to convince ourselves that ours is a sure thing, we must put out of our minds the evidence that argues against it. But that is the very evidence we'd want to keep in mind as we move forward. If you decide to start your business but then throw away the arguments against it, pretending that your business is a sure thing, you'll be throwing away precious information you gleaned the hard way worrying by night and researching by day. You know creative people who get a hunch, turn it into dogma, and then guided by it fly blindly with no capacity to re-chart their course. They've gone blind to other perspectives, cocksure but dangerous, or at least no fun to be with, because they're so pig-headed.

Still, if we keep the reasons against our choice in mind they may send us back into hem-haw or ping-pong. You also know creative, thoughtful people who never get off the dime because the red flags paralyze them. Besides ignoring the red flags is a virtual necessity when selling your new business concept to potential allies—partners, investors, suppliers, and customers. Painting an exclusively rosy scenario for them will garner more support than handing them some turnkey argument that your venture is a turkey.

Cocksure. Can't live with it, can't live without it. We're damned if you ignore the red flags, but also damned if we obsess about them.

There still remains a fourth option. It is the one that doesn't have us holding out for black-and-white certainty.

Sure enough: Face the doubt and place the bet anyway. Start the business but call it a bet. Constrain the temptation to tell yourself exclusively affirming stories about the bet you've placed. Don't burn the quadrants carrying the arguments for the path not taken. Knowing that it's a bet, but that bets are all we get, you hold your uncertainty in such a way as to not be paralyzed by it. Indeed, you'll still use the rosy scenarios to win friends and influence people, but you won't slide into mistaking your reassuring rhetoric for certainty. In private moments, like in bed at night, you remember the red flags. They don't freak you out as much because you've learned how to face doubt and recognize your doubts as old familiar bedbugs. Your doubts are still there, and yet they don't send you lurching in search of greener grass.

Knowing doubt better and having learned to be able to live with it, you recognize that the grass is brownish-green everywhere. It's brownish-green and still you can't help but try to find the most green and least brown among your options. You look, but you don't hold out for pure, pristine, golf-course kelly green anymore, not holding out for it actually makes you less perturbable, which makes you more reliable to friends and colleagues. You can attend to your bets on the patch of ground you've staked out for yourself, aware of, but not distracted by, the fact that there are other bets you could have taken, bets that could have even proved more green in the end. This is what it means to be sure enough. Sure enough is an under-appreciated option. It is the mature decision-maker's creed. You should always strive for sure enough.

Or should you?

Before we subscribe to an absolute—one with which we have a very limited capacity to comply—we must ask, why, if the sure enough approach is so sound, do people take that approach only sometimes and indeed more rarely than they take the other approaches? Why, if it's so much better, does it need to be argued for?

Well, maybe because it takes a long time to wean ourselves off the naïve childhood dream of a sure thing. Maybe we were too long accommodated by our protective parents who, in our formative years, fed us a fantasy that certainty could be had in this world. But it's more than that. People have their reasons and to get at them, there's another way to think about the four approaches to dealing with doubt.

We humans live in two worlds—our inner world of thought and feeling and the outer world in which we act. We can be decisive in either, neither, or both. That gives us four possible states. These, it turns out, correspond to our four ways of making decisions.

Hem-haw is being uncertain both inside and out, and waiting until certainty arises. *Ping-pong* is sure on the inside—always emphatic but not always about the same thing, which to the outside world appears indecisive. *Sure enough* is being unsure inside but acting decisively outside. And *cocksure* is the full alignment—all systems go.

		Outer world	
		Indecisive	Decisive
Inner World	Sure	Ping-pong	Cock-sure
	Unsure	Hem-haw	Sure Enough

And upon further examination, it's clear that these four states are really stages, stepping stones along the path toward making a decision—any kind of decision.

Facing an uncertainty, we first hem and haw. We're undecided which is perfectly reasonable. And it pays to stay in hem-haw sometimes to see if a decision is really necessary. If we do have to make a decision, then we consider each alternative. To really consider an option you have to get into it and really test-drive it, imagining what it would be like to choose it, because half-hearted consideration of an option may not make it real enough to provide a full evaluation of its merits. That's ping-ponging.

At some point one of the options feels slightly better than the other, or you run out of time and you have to commit to a choice, even though you may still feel doubt. Here, you've entered sure enough.

And then, eventually you make peace with your choice and move on, by treating it as complete. You commit your heart to the decision you had to make. To harvest as much as possible from the choice you've made you convince yourself that you chose the best option. That's cocksure.

Making the most of what makes up your mind is therefore not a matter of employing only one of the four approaches. Rather it's a matter of being curious about the relationship among them— their sequence, your own decision-making style, your range of flexibility in adjusting your style for improvement. It starts with an appreciation of the benefits and costs of each state.

Hem-hawing costs time, energy, and social status. The longer you spend not knowing and not acting the more it costs. Still the longer you spend in it, the greater the possibility you won't have to decide at all. The early bird gets the worm, but sometimes the late bird doesn't have to eat a worm at all. Decisions sometimes make themselves, a better option comes along, or you get over the dilemma altogether.

Ping-ponging also costs. But convincing yourself as completely as possible of one option and then the other is a great way to give each option its best chance of proving its worth and you may be able to shortcut your decision if one option proves convincing enough.

Sure enough feels like a transition state. You've made your decision, why are you still doubting? But it is also the most realistic depiction of what a made decision is. It is a bet.

Cocksure is the ideal state—the state of doubt-free action, but it's ideal only when the action you have chosen is one that will pay off. Otherwise it's among the most dangerous states of all. Wholeheartedly believing in something wrong—that's when we make our greatest mistakes.

Different decisions and decision-makers pass through this sequence at different paces. Unconscious decisions and unconscious decision-makers zip ASAP to cocksure. Fence sitters dwell as long as possible in the Hem-haw or Ping-pong states. Discomfort with inner uncertainty compels some people to cling to cocksure at all costs.

To dance well with doubt, consider a real dancer. A professional dancer needs both fluency and fluidity. Fluency means having a complete repertoire of postures or positions. Fluidity means the flexibility to move between them gracefully, comfortable in any state and comfortable changing between states. To make the most of what makes up your mind you need something similar: comfort with each state, the versatility to be able to move among them. Fluent and fluid dancers gained their skill by using their practice time well, concentrating on the moves that come hardest, rather than spending time repeating what comes easy. So among these decision-making stages, which comes hardest?

In three out of four states—hem-haw, ping-pong, and cocksure—we eschew doubt. These are the most popular states. Most of us need more practice with sure enough.

Doubt is taxing. Most of us try to move out of it as soon as possible. Doubt takes a huge amount of practice. It's like learning to stand on the tips of your toes in ballet. When in doubt you can almost hear the meter ticking and your resources draining.

We'd rather not answer tough judgment calls, but instead hope the ringing will stop and the call will go away. The outer world often won't let us off the hook that easily. It demands decisiveness and so we comply. The people around you encourage you to get over it, make up your mind, and get reliable. Decisiveness sells. We need to look certain in order to convince others to join us.

We even need to look certain in order to convince ourselves. You know the sound of someone trying to convince himself of a decision he has made, vigorously fork-editing and reminding himself over and over of the merits of the thing he's stuck with and the insignificance of what he's stuck giving up. The frequency with which people try to convince themselves of decisions they've made is evidence that we're not very comfortable with sure enough. You place a bet and want a sign from the universe that you've chosen well. Unless and until the universe comes through with that sign, what are you going to do? Do without? Not if you can help it, and you can. If the universe isn't going to shout what you need to hear, you'll shout it instead, find, hire, or befriend people who will shout the encouragement you need. We say what we need to hear, especially when no one around us will say it for us. The louder the doubt rings in your head and heart, the more you might be inclined to insist publicly that you are sure about what you are doing.

There's a strong tendency therefore to move toward cocksure faster or more completely than is good for our health. And to counter that, to the extent we can we need to cultivate doubt-tolerance, which like drought tolerance is the capacity to withstand dry periods when the universe is not sending you juicy endorsement. The Buddhists have a saying, "Though my heart is on fire, my eyes are cold as ashes." It's a mantra for the sure enough and a very hard state to maintain.

What helps is knowing doubts inside and out, being able to picture all four quadrants at once, and for that we'll set the stage with a quick survey of wondering's long history, and then dig into the wonderings themselves.

A Natural History of Wondering in Four Acts

It's hard to accurately encapsulate billions of years of evolution into a few paragraphs. What follows therefore will be dense, figurative, and impressionistic. No worries. Just capture the occasional gist as it washes over you and it will put your personal relationship with doubt in an interesting long-view perspective.

Act One: Wondering Without a Wonderer

The wonders have been a problem for life since the beginning, but for the longest time, no creatures personally wondered. Instead Mother Nature—who is not a person, though it is convenient to think of her as one—passively accumulated tools that enabled creatures to address them.

Silently and in a billion creatures at once, Mother Nature sifted through candidate biological adaptations the way a miller sifts grain through a sieve, separating the useful from the useless. The useful adaptations confer wisdom—the guiding wherewithal by which creatures address their tough judgment calls, the wisdom to know and act upon the difference where the difference matters. Though now we pursue the wisdom by a variety of other means, at core, the wisdom we seek is the same as it ever was. Since the beginning life has, in effect, wondered what to do.

Darwin called Mother Nature's sieve *selection* (as in *natural selection*). By it he meant the totality of conditions that must be met by a body in order to survive. The tools that successfully pass through Mother Nature's sifting process are the ones that help a body get by—not just survive but survive long enough to pass on the tools to offspring in subsequent sifting. The tools that pass through the sieve accumulate in some creature's genetic memory to be re-sifted with every generation of that creature's descendants.

Mother Nature's sieve is at its core a simple trial-and-error process whereby she test-drives wisdom and the best tools win. The term "trial and error" is shorthand for something like candidates, test, and winners. It's funny that trial and error includes the error, which for productivity's sake may seem the least appealing part of the process. Error may be in "trial and error" precisely because it is the most counter-intuitive part of the process. It is very hard for us to wrap our minds around the fact that producing masterpieces entails producing some error, an important reason why it took so long for biologist to figure out how natural selection worked. For a long time before Darwin people assumed that God made creatures the way a master baker

47

bakes pies. No burnt ones, no error. A codfish makes 40 million eggs to produce a single offspring. That's counter-intuitive.

Trial-and-error processes work in the presence of three conditions: something to judge the trials (*e.g.*, the sieve of natural selection), some candidates to bring to trial (*e.g.*, the multitude of grains or candidate adaptations), and something that the successful trials win (*e.g.*, a place in genetic memory). Mother Nature isn't a single force therefore, but rather a trinity of three forces. Here they are, complete with nicknames:

Lax: (AKA the candidates, variation, the grains of possibility)

Lax is the loose pool of possible adaptations from which Axe picks the best.

Axe: (AKA the judge, selection, the sieve)

Axe is the one who gives some candidates the axe and lets some candidates pass through. Axe makes the cut, winnowing out the grains that don't confer wisdom for dealing with life's wonders.

Ox: (AKA memory, retention, winnowing's winnings)

Ox grants the winners perpetual life—retaining them as stubbornly and persistently as an ox for use again and again, or at least until they stop working.

While collectively productive, these three forces work at cross-purposes to each other. Lax is loose and inclusive, ready to try anything and everything. Axe is just the opposite, ruthlessly selective, holding to high standards. If an adaptation doesn't work, it's out of here. If a creature's toolkit doesn't cut it, the creature is cleared off the stage. Ox wants to keep everything, but Axe won't let him. Ox wants to keep things the same, but Lax is always trying out new things. Between Lax's and Axe's entropic and erosive powers, Ox's efforts to keep things the same are somewhat thwarted. Genetic memory is no pack rat. It forgets what isn't useful the way we forget math when we don't use it. Genes retain only what's necessary, which means they forget whatever they rely upon something in their environment to remember, the way we might forget the math that we expect calculators, our bookkeepers, or our spouses to handle readily on our behalf. It's not how Ox would have it. He would prefer to keep everything, but he doesn't always get his way.

Born of the tension between Lax, Ox and Axe, life arrived with dilemmas from the get-go. And the dilemmas aren't unlike the dilemmas we still face. Have you ever written by committee? You've got your lax, all-inclusive types who keep adding colorful bits; your persnickety Axe-editor types who'll cut the heart out of your precious prose without even flinching; and you've got your Ox-retentive types who say, "Leave it. It's all right as it is." Even creating something by yourself, you've probably heard from Lax, Axe, and Ox. They live in all of us.

A closer look at Lax: What are these grains that get filtered through Mother Nature's sieve?

If they were the same grains over and over then evolution wouldn't have much capacity to add innovation, so obviously a pinch of new grain gets added in each generation, but from where? It's long been thought that the inventive part of nature is the occasional chance mutation—out-of-the-blue trait that passes with flying colors through natural selection's sieve. What we're coming to realize is that most innovation happens through variation on tools that already work. Tools that have worked in the past are likely to continue to work and moreover to work well for other tasks too. With a little modification a nice pair of fins makes a nice pair of wings, legs, or arms. Contrary to popular reputation, evolution is more about keeping and building upon what works than it is about inventing new things from scratch.

To the extent that evolution is about building new things it mostly does so by recombining existing things that have worked. A tool that successfully passes through Mother Nature's filter can merge with other tools. They combine at random, but not just with any other possible adaptation. Rather, they combine with other winners that also succeeded in passing through the sieve. They make the kind of productive merger deals that get made at class reunions at the finest schools where the most productive students schmooze and pool resources. This makes for the best of the best—a hearty bowl of Cream of the Crop Soup, with three cooks—lax, axe and ox—stirring the broth.

But setting aside these attempts at intuitive personification, notice this: For years, living things didn't care whether their adaptations passed through natural selection's sieve. A microbe whose adaptations got passed on to the next generation was as enthusiastic about its success as a grain is enthusiastic about being small enough to pass through a sieve. To this day, microbes still don't feel elation when their adaptations pass through the sieve, because they have no sense of delight or disappointment with which to feel elation. They don't think, "Hurray, I made it!" when they pass on their genetic toolkits to their offspring because they still have no sense of self with which to be self-congratulating. Mushrooms, plants, algae . . . a lot of life is like that, wholly reliant on Mother Nature's trial–and-error process to do the wondering that enables them to address the world's tough calls.

Some aspects of being human remain like that. Much of the time, your body's tools do their own thing without your conscious input, interference, or, as can sometimes be embarrassing, your control. You didn't choose your body, you inherited it, already equipped with tools that have sifted down through an inconceivable number of generations of trial-and-error sifting.

But unlike trees and fungi that take what they get passively, neither impressed nor disappointed by their pot-luck accumulation, you've got feelings about what you've got. How did you get that way? That's act two.

Take It Personally (T.I.P.)

"Though you didn't make yourself, they're holding you responsible, so act as though you did."

Some people will tell you that you are your body; others will tell you that you are your mind controlling your body. Either way they won't let you forget it, because somebody's got to be held responsible for your body's actions or else the world would be in quite a fix.

So long as you are young, healthy, smart, friendly, civilized, thin, and good-looking, it's easy to uphold the belief that you are your body or your body's boss. It's a little harder when your body starts acting up on you.

Take some comfort from an evolutionary perspective: Your body is the product of organic processes that aren't designed to make you happy, but rather to bring you biological reproductive success. The biological adaptations you've got are what they are, not because they won a popularity contest with you and your ancestors who passed them on to you, but because they fit through the openings created by the sieve of natural selection.

The evolutionary approach suggests that we didn't make ourselves. If instead we are the product of a trial-and-error winnowing process, then why hold us responsible for how we behave? Some people think it's dangerous to have people running around armed with the excuse that they didn't make themselves. "'I'm an axe-murderer but it's not my fault.' We have enough trouble as is with Twinkie defenses. We don't need more excuses." They therefore try to ignore our evolutionary origins focusing more optimistically on how experience shapes us. But that doesn't help much. Did you choose your parents? Did they choose theirs? If people need a way to shift blame off themselves, they find it, regardless of whether evolutionary theory supplies one.

Still, it does seem unreasonable to hold people responsible for what they didn't choose. The more society cares about fairness and the more evidence scientists amass suggesting that bad choices often have biological and neurological causes, the harder it is for us to credibly hold people responsible for who they happen to be.

Is your body a biological machine or a person who decides and must pay the price for its choices? The answer is yes to both—therefore, a simple pearl of wisdom: distinguish between exculpation (freedom from guilt) and exoneration (freedom from responsibility). Exculpation is your birthright; exoneration is not. You are free from guilt but not responsibility. You did not make you, but somebody has to be held responsible for you nonetheless, so by default you win.

Does this formulation change anything? Not much. You'll still feel like a creep when you've done something wrong. You'll still pay the price and reap the benefit for all the bets you place.

But at a subtle level, there are advantages to making this distinction. It does relieve some of the burden of self-chastisement and that can increase your compassion for yourself and others in ways that make self-improvement paradoxically easier.

If every time you see a disappointing side of yourself you wince, there's a good chance that eventually you'll stop seeing that disappointing side of yourself. If you know that you didn't make you or your predicament, you may be able to keep looking until you find a way to work with who you are more effectively.

Often when we do something wrong, we scold ourselves, like the stern parent who knows better. There is probably some self-governing benefit to this, but next time you do it give equal time to that person inside of you who's being scolded. Apologize to yourself out loud and with dignity for your error. Give some explanation to yourself for the mistake—one that doesn't free you from responsibility but does free you from blame of authorship. Take a little comfort from exculpation.

And while taking comfort, give some too. No one else chose what he or she was given either. Think of how shocking it must be for the people who look down at what they've become and find nothing from their wish list. They too are not their own authors. They too are held responsible nonetheless.

Act Two: Once More with Feeling

Remember when you were a kid imagining what you would do if you were granted three wishes? Of course you'd use at least one wish to wish for more wishes. In a way, that is what life did about a billion years ago. After billions of years of trial-and-error trawling for good adaptations it netted a nifty new tool, a tool-trawling tool—formed out of sentience, the feeling of pleasure and pain, and a way to record what behaviors caused which sensation. Like the biological process from which this new tool came, it too operates by trial and error to accumulate adaptive learning for dealing with life's dilemmas. Do something that hurts, and you won't do it again. Do something pleasurable, and you'll go back for more.

It's as though Mother Nature's trial-and-error process for solving dilemmas stumbled upon a way of making a miniature version of itself for creatures to carry around in their bodies. Feeling even has its own mini-trinity:

Lax: The broad variety of behaviors you try out before you find out what hurts.

Axe: The sensation of pleasure and pain, which in effect judges the behaviors you try out in the world, and gives the axe to any behaviors that cause you pain.

Ox: The somewhat stubborn retention of tried and truly pleasurable behaviors worth repeating.

If you were granted one wish for more wishes, you'd use its additional wishes to satisfy the same desires you'd satisfy with your other two original wishes. Similarly, feelings select for the same kinds of things natural selection would choose, or at least it did in the beginning. The pleasures of eating, sex, nurturing children, and being nurtured all aid in getting our adaptations passed on to our offspring.

As an adaptive tool, sentience is definitely a keeper. Equipped with it, a being is able to pass through Mother Nature's sieve more effectively. With this tool, a creature could learn within its lifetime, adjusting itself on the fly to the shape of local consequence. A creature with feelings could acquire new tools within a lifetime, like a grain that could correct itself mid-course as it headed toward Mother Nature's sieve anticipating and adjust itself in midair to angle and dive right through for safe passage.

If you saw a grain do this, you'd say that it looked like it intended to get through the sieve, and indeed, creatures with feeling are life's first intentional beings, looking out for themselves, with an internalized appetite to make the right choices because they feel better than wrong ones. Bugs, fish, lizards, frogs, bats, all sorts of animals . . . a lot of living beings are guided by the combination of biologically accumulated adaptations from act one, and the fine-tuning adaptations that come through the trial-and-error learning that happens through feeling.

And of course to a large extent we humans find our way by feel too. Above almost everything else, what drives us is the pursuit of pleasure and avoidance of pain. We have this in common with all sentient beings. But in us humans not all feeling is aligned with what's good for survival and reproduction. Something has changed. Something is different about us and that leads to act three.

But before heading on, take a moment to pay homage to trial and error. This simple process turns out to be deeply fundamental to life. Trial and error with all it implies is at the root of all adaptation and learning. If there were anyway to pinpoint what life force is, trial and error would be it. It distinguishes the inanimate from the animate. With trial and error, life can systematically increase the fit between itself and its environment. Trial and error is the most amazing commonplace we ever ignore, so it's nice to stop occasionally to appreciate it.

Take It Personally (T.I.P.):

I am a trial in a trial-and-error process.

Evolution is a marathon brainstorming session. Lots of trial balloons get floated and the ones that succeed tend to proliferate. Your choices, ideas, decisions and bets are trial balloons too. Therefore, put your weight behind them, but also hold them somewhat lightly. Let your balloons sink when it's time. Build them to last 100 years, but be ready to let them go tomorrow.

This is sound if somewhat hackneyed advice. People always say you should not become too emotionally involved with your ideas. If that's such good advice, why do people need to be reminded of it?

Because it is hard advice to follow. Feelings are very credible with us humans. If they weren't credible, they wouldn't be effective guidance for dealing with the wonderings of the world. Feelings are like a pre-screening of your contributions to the cosmic brainstorm, helping you sift through trials in your head before you try them out in the real world.

Feeling's pre-screening comes to your rescue even in conventional brainstorming sessions at the office. Even though the facilitator tells you to blurt any idea that comes to mind, no one ever really does. The discomfort you get when imagining blurting some ideas keeps you from floating them. The comfort of other ideas makes you willing to float them.

Feelings enable you to bet well on which ideas to float in life's brainstorming session. But even when you bet well, some ideas that you float will still be sinkers. When your bets come out badly it hurts. And likewise when your idea wins, you'll feel great.

No wonder we are emotionally invested in our trial balloons. If we weren't, we'd float any idea without caring one whit what happens to it.

Next time one of your ideas sinks, and indeed next time one floats to the highest heights, remember that they are all trials in a trial-and-error process and that the sinking bad or swimmingly good feelings we have about our ideas are an essential part of the process that leads to the best ideas getting tried.

Act Three: Now Showing in a Theater Inside You

Which came first, consciousness or life? It's anyone's guess . . . and everyone's. There's no conclusive evidence, but people often insist they know.

Many people say that consciousness came first. A God Consciousness that takes in the whole picture. All-seeing, all-knowing, already having all the right answers to the wonders that still bug us mortals.

Well, consciousness—what is that thing anyway, besides something we revere? Like any word, it's whatever we agree to say it is. Its meaning is in the eye of the beholder. With a lot of words there's strong consensus among the beholders. Other words are interpreted more widely and confusingly: *consciousness* is one of these.

Let's say it means an ability to see the big picture, or at least some of the big picture. By this definition, the more of the big picture that a creature sees; the more conscious it is. By this definition, whose toolkit includes consciousness, aside from the God we picture in our mind's eye?

If anyone's does it's yours, and where this consciousness resides is in your mind's eye itself. Your mind's eye can picture a lot—galaxies, atoms, new friends, friends long dead, things you haven't tried yet, and things you had better not try.

Potato bugs don't seem to take in much of the big picture. We can guess that their awareness of galaxies and friends long dead is less detailed than ours. And that's OK. They don't mind. The less consciousness you have, the less you miss it.

The mind's eye is like a movie theater inside your head. You are a movie-making creature with a vast capacity to picture what isn't front and center. The degree of detail in your mental movies surpasses that of any other known creature. How long have we had the capacity to do this mental movie making? At most, about 50,000 years, which is nothing in 3.5 billion. Why we have it, why we do when other creatures don't, and how we got it is a long story some of which remains a mystery. But we've got it in spades, which makes us pioneers, prototyping an altogether new wisdom generating system. But in another way, the mind's eye is more of the same trial–and-error sifting, another mini-trinity of Lax, Axe and Ox working in the cognitive arena:

Lax: The big loose and ever growing archive of footage in your mental movie warehouse.

Axe: The mind's movie editor, selecting from among the available footage the pieces it deems relevant.

Ox: The part of your mind that having pictured enough says, "OK, that's a wrap," and translates from movie to real-world action.

For example, you're going along and suddenly you find yourself at a fork in the road, maybe a real one on a real road, maybe one you picture in your mind. Either way you start imagining what would happen if you took one or the other option at the fork. By mixing and matching mental movie footage you are able to run alternative scenarios in your mind's eye. You sift through the scenarios for the one that fits the outcome you want, and then it's lights, camera, action—you act out the chosen scene in the real world. Very convenient this—with a mental movie studio, you don't have to try everything out in the real world to discover the consequences.

Whereas bacteria, plants, and fungi have only biology's one sifter accumulating guidance for dealing with the wonderings, and animals have two sifters, instinct and feeling, you now have three, like three wise counselors using one method, trial and error, in three different mediums—genes, feelings and thoughts—for accumulating wisdom. All of them have your ear. But they are not in complete agreement about what you should do. What the body and the mind want can be at cross-purposes. Sometimes, one man's pleasure is the same man's poison. This explains some of the human ambivalence we touched on earlier.

Having all three wise counselors, you have to deal with some particularly human kinds of uncertainty. It can make you envy simpler creatures who, without our extraordinary mind's eye abilities, have one less source to guide them and therefore seem to have an easier time knowing what to do. Trees never look uncertain. Fish rarely do. But by mid-life you have wrinkles on your forehead no fish will ever possess. They signify your membership in a special club of advanced doubters who suffer not from a lack of good guidance but from having too much.

Take It Personally (T.I.P.)
We didn't fall from grace, we rose from slime.

There has been a lot of hand wringing lately about humans and where we went wrong. Was it Western culture? Capitalism? Money? Stupid white men? Something made us "un-natural."

It's true, we have new unique problems; some of them are extremely hairy. But these new problems are no mistake; they arise from our natural-though-unprecedented abilities.

All life forms expediently expand their domains to consume as many resources as they can. When a species stumbles by trial and error upon an adaptation that enables them to exploit resources, they make the most of it. Their population expands, they consume more, or even waste more, just as humans do. We are no greedier than the rest; we are just much better at exploiting resources, largely because our mental movie-making ability is just the kind of adaptation that enables us to do so.

Nor are we more nearsighted than other creatures. In fact, with our ability to map out possible futures with mental movies, we can foresee the future far more capably than any other creature. Without mental movie making, we wouldn't have the capacity to imagine a grace from which we might have fallen.

It may be useful to imagine a more idyllic time and wiser creatures that lived in it. One advantage of any idealization is that it gives you something to aspire to, in fact, a mind's-eye movie of the state you want to read. But don't sell yourself short. The ancients knew less than you do which must have made deciding what to do much easier.

Act Four: Finally, an "I" to Wonder

When you say, "I wonder," you are employing a brand-spanking-new tool, even newer than the mind's eye: a mind's eye picture of yourself. Close your eyes. See yourself? That's the one. Your ability to do that is at most about 20,000 years old, very new and coming on stronger and stronger with every recent decade.

Your mind's I. The lead character in most, if not all, of your mental movies, dominating the action whether it's on-screen or off—the point of view, number one to look out for, the subject of so many of your sentences, the seat of your soul, the center of your universe, the one stable point in a whirling world.

Having an I is itself a source of great new guidance you rely upon daily when dealing with the Wonders. *"Should I quit?" "Am I being to wishy-washy?"* The I pops up everywhere and sticks around to enforce your decisions. When you say, "I'm a TV repair man," you are holding yourself to a decision you made a while ago to become one. "I wouldn't do that." "I'm going to become a doctor." "I love you." "I" signs contracts between you and others, but also between you and yourself.

And yet how constant is it? You know what it is like to feel very different in the presence of different kinds of people. With your parents you may feel like a child; with your children, like your parents. We maintain a sense that the self is constant, even if it isn't constant.

Your sense of self, like all other guidance is an adaptation evolving by trial and error—new guidance, new medium, but the same trial-and-error process, with its three cooks constantly stirring the simmering pot.

Lax supplies the loose collection of all your possible self-images: the footage you've accumulated in your warehouse about yourself—the selves you remember having been, selves others have seen you as being, selves that by analogy to other people are what you imagine yourself being, with dread, ambition, hope and delusion. None of them are complete selves, but nonetheless they conspire and fill in for each other to give you the impression of self-consciousness, consciousness or whole-picture perspective on your totality.

Axe screens these self-images both internally and externally, for example, in the company of someone who is like you—how you'll begin to feel more likeable as though their impression filtered out some aspects of who you might be, letting other aspects shine through; how their impression can leave a lasting impression, the way that in a moment of disappointment with yourself you might hear the voice of a parent, grandparent, teacher, boss or ex-spouse who used to scold you.

Ox accumulates the relatively constant aspects of your self-image, the versions of who you are that are evoked most frequently because of your roles, responsibilities, plans, and the social expectations of the people with whom you spend the most time.

Earlier we discussed the power of analogy in dealing with doubt and the importance of deciding which analogies were most apt, because analogies guide us in decision making. In act one of this brief natural history we saw how genes make new adaptations by recombining and reconfiguring preexisting tools, and here we could draw an analogy between the mixing and matching of genes and the mixing and matching of movie footage to get a vast variety of possible guidance for dealing with judgment calls. In act three we discussed the ways that mental movies are formed by splicing together footage in mix-and-match combinations, which is how analogical thinking happens. And now in act four we notice that images of the self are also a collage, footage spliced together in ever shifting combinations, some of which certainly is like analogy. In the presence of Aunt Judith, you find yourself feeling like a medley: your father plus some TV comedian, plus your past self. Something she says reminds you of someone else, who by analogy you also assume you have become.

In biology, Axe is natural selection, filtering or selecting for biological reproductive success. In sentience, Axe selects for behaviors that confer pleasure. So in mental movie making and in self-image on the mind's silver screen, what is Axe selecting for? This gets complicated, but it is a crucial determinant of how we manage tough judgment calls and what kinds of decisions we make. It relates to our earlier admonition to choose analogies carefully. But by what standard?

The answer is very complex, but a short version of it goes something like this. Fit. The mind's eye seeks footage that fits in context. But which context? Well, by now, with biological adaptations, feelings, and a whole warehouse full of memory, to say nothing of a huge real world and a rich culture, fitting with existing context means many things.

Most of us select for footage that fits with and engenders pleasure and avoid to the extent we can footage that fits with and evokes pain. Some of us can't help but think painful thoughts, but few of us prefer to. Many of us when making decisions avoid considering certain scenarios, not because they are unlikely to play out but because they feel bad. Self-delusion is largely an expression of how much our movie making is biased by our pleasure-seeking guidance. "A legend in his own mind" is someone who thinks he's brilliant not because it is accurate but because it feels good.

To some extent, all of us select for footage that fits in context with other existing footage. We require a degree of congruity and consistency in our viewing and feel funny when we come upon an inconsistency. Of course if it feels funny enough it won't fit with what feels good—the other standard we just discussed—so one option is to ignore it. All of us have blind spots where we don't see our double standards operate because it doesn't feel good.

All of us to some degree also select for footage that fits the context of the mental movies that others around are viewing. Even what you think of as 'outside the box,' is only interesting because it is within the box of your cultural context. Anything truly outside the box would be perceived as pure nonsense.

And of course we select for footage that fits in context of reality—the real world outside of ourselves. We generally talk to each other as though this is the only appropriate or important selective standard for fitness that matters, as though we are all realists merely seeking the truth. We certainly are, in large part because mental movie footage that accurately fits reality tends to be useful. It tends to help us make good decisions. But this is not an absolute. For one thing, the world is extraordinarily complex and none of us can afford to chase down accuracy into all its details. We use sketches of what's accurate. Also a lot of "reality" has always been and continues to remain in a realm of speculation. The more speculative the question, the more other kinds of fit matter in selecting footage. Since, for example, the origins of the universe remain a speculative matter, we tend to fill in the gap with footage that fits in context by other standards — by what feels good or what proves useful, whether accurate or not. So you see it depends.

Here's an example of the mind's eye axe and what fits its selective standards.

Acts three and four have involved an analogy to movie making. Most of us have at least a vague sense of how it's done, so right here we're mixing and matching, splicing a piece of mental movie footage about the film-making process into a mental movie about how the mind works.

But really, is the mind's eye like a movie theater inside your head? There's something wrong with that picture.

Who is watching the movies you play? A little "you" inside your head? But what goes on inside this little "you"? Does it have a little person inside its head too? It can't go on forever like nested boxes. Something in there has eventually got to do some viewing or else this whole notion of the mind's eye theater cannot be accurate.

Here's another thing wrong with it: This central star of your inner movies is nowhere to be found. Neuroscientists, scholars, philosophers, scientists, theologians, psychiatrists, medical doctors have looked for it everywhere and they can't find it. Many still assert its existence but we haven't a clue where it resides. You could lop parts off a person all day and night, and he'd still feel as though he had a central self, poor thing, all the way up to the moment when he lost his consciousness, the mental movie maker. After that, we might still think the person is there, but the person in question would no longer think it.

Whatever it is about the picture of mind's eye theater that makes it so intuitive and familiar, like the kind of footage we get out of the warehouse frequently, it's not being selected first and foremost for its fit with reality. The reality about our sense of self remains speculative, and so we think that what is useful feels consistent with experience, with cultural standards, and perhaps with the kind of pleasure we take in feeling as though we are in command at the helm of our personal space bridges minding the monitors.

Indeed as long as you have "consciousness," you can hold constant the idea that you are constant without having to be constant. All it takes is a little film footage that you pull out and attach to pretty much everything. The footage is of you being constant. Ultimately this may violate the mind's eye standards for internal consistency, but as we've seen with the mind's eye theater, internal consistency is only one of many standards. It can be relaxed in favor of other standards. Fitting into a culture that depends upon you to be consistent and assumes that you are may be far more important.

Thinking we are constant feels very useful but is not conducive to accurately discovering our place in the universe. Trying to describe the universe while holding our "true selves" as absolute is like trying to describe the motion of the galaxies while holding the earth still in the center of it all. The mathematical modeling gets convoluted very quickly.

If you ever want keep yourself up at night, meditate on your eventual demise. We are *mirror mortals*, aware of our mortality because we can make mental models of the worst thing that will ever happen to us personally, our own deaths. Potato bugs don't worry about death because they don't see it coming. But by making mental models of the future, we see death coming from miles off. Some of us can't help it though it is unpleasant to imagine. Others of us are perfectly capable of finding more happy-fitting thoughts for long stretches.

Anthropologists often mark the birth of the modern human mind with the beginning of ritual burial. For the first time a living thing was fussing over the loss of self. The obsession with the self's death lives on in us. Where does the *I* go when the body dies? It's not a question the dead ponder. The living do, forcing sense from life with *I* as its most basic assumption.

In spite of our inability to locate the core self, we rely upon it all the time. It is so important to us, so useful that we can hardly imagine time before or after it's supposed existence. The *I*'s existence is perhaps the most frequently visited of our mental movies—a piece of footage you attach to most circumstances. Why? Because it is so darn useful in addressing the wonderings of the world. It opens up vast new sources of wisdom and ways to retain it. It helps you deal with the wonderings of the ancient world, but it also generates a whole set of new wonders tailored to our peculiarly modern human world.

We have come to rely upon this impression of a constant self as our anchor in a sea of doubt. You've surely met people who think they are being consistent when they aren't. To some extent we all do this—as much as we can get away with without getting called on it or violating our own standards for internal consistency.

Take It Personally (T.I.P.)
I think, therefore I think I am.

Some spiritual teachers say that the "I" isn't real and that you should therefore get over your royal I-ness. Sounds good on paper, but in reality, that's more reality than any of us are really capable of keeping in mind. The world in which you are not the central character may be a useful place to visit occasionally, but you can't take up residence there, so let yourself off the hook. Get with the program. Enjoy your "I" while you've got it.

And when you're finally at death's door and have to surrender it, it is quite possible that you won't miss it any more than potato bugs miss theirs.

Other spiritual teachers suggest that you should plumb your depths to get in touch with your true core self. Perhaps part of the appeal of that advice is that it fits so snugly in context with our intuitive sense of the mind's eye movie watcher inside the movie watcher inside the movie watcher, etc., like peeling the onion to get to the bottom of things. It could be useful advice even if it is unlikely that there is a core self. It depends a lot on what your "outer self" pictures this inner self to be like. Probably, what we call getting to the core self is more like adding layers of self-reference rather than peeling off layers of anything. You make a mental movie of yourself making a mental movie of yourself making a mental movie of yourself—not very core, though perhaps very useful.

Reincarnation fits resoundingly well with our pretty universal impression of the self as stable and constant. Given what we now know about the ways life evolve, it is disappointingly difficult to come up with a reasonable sounding model whereby souls float from an old body to a new one. But you couldn't find a better fitting story to go along with the self as central. The problem is just that it gets as messy and convoluted as pre-Copernican astronomy. Another version of reincarnation may be a bit more accurate, though more vague. It's the one in which life force merges into one great pool after we die and reconfigures into other living things. Organic matter does tend to recycle, but that version will have little appeal to a constant self.

All is not lost, not even for that in each of us that can't stand the thought of leaving no trace of the soul behind. It's those sieves we pass through and what gets retained in the process. Your genetic memories live on in your children. And your movie footage lives on too in your brainchildren. Mental movies aren't just for show. They lead to action that leaves a lasting impression on your survivors. How lasting? Well it's sort of a trial–and-error process out there. Yes, culture too has its sieve or sieves. Lax supplies tons of ideas, products, symbols, and creations; culture selectively retains some and forgets others. Culture plods on carrying forward whatever has proven useful in the past. And personal culture, the people whose lives you touched, rest assured you will reincarnate in them. If how you regard your friends shapes how they regard themselves, then that effect persists after you die. What reincarnates are the effects of the deeds you've done in your wonderful life. Very few of these will be credited to you, but that won't reduce their power one whit, and besides you won't care by then.

Jeremy Sherman

The Seven Wonderings of the Ancient World

The world is mysterious in so many ways it would be impossible to come up with a definitive set of categories within which the mysteries neatly fall. The following wonderings, both of the ancient and modern worlds, should not be taken too literally. There are, no doubt more than these 14. They are all interconnected, so it is hard to comb out the strands into non-overlapping categories, and in real life a doubt you experience could be manifestations of multiple wonderings at once.

The ancient wonderings are with us today. To make them as relevant as possible we'll focus mostly on the way they manifest for you. Still, we'll include some description of how they operate in nonhuman life. And with the wonderings of the modern world, we'll describe the ways in which they are uniquely human.

The First Wondering of the Ancient World:

Should I Join This?

Big Bang theorists and Hindus say that the universe was once a unified whole, perfectly harmonized, all one. But, say the Hindus, that was too boring, so it exploded into many separate things that now configure in endlessly fascinating ways, coming together and coming apart, moving into each other's spheres of influence and moving out. That's when the fun started—and wondering number one: Who, what, where, how, and when to connect, what's worth connecting to, and what isn't. Figuring this out has been at the top of Mother Nature's to-do list since the very beginning and all along.

There's no life without selective association. Organic molecules have selective affinities. Selectively permeable cell membranes let some molecules in and not others, enzymes bind some molecules and bounce off others, immune systems selectively welcome and selectively attack your body's visitors, predator/prey, parasite/host, mating and rejecting. From your proteins to pores, our bodies are gatekeeping geniuses.

Our minds are too. Unconsciously and every day you make millions of decisions about what to move toward and what to pass up. You make multitudes more of these decisions right than wrong.

But do you remember a time when you said "Yes" to a union you should have turned down or "No" to a union you should have made? Of course, and you probably spent some time regretting it too. And do you remember every time you got it right—every good deal you made and every bad deal you passed up? Of course not. Your capacity to ignore what's working is working.

The questionable unions that rise to consciousness and keep you up at night whirring in active mental movie-making mode are the dilemmas, the A.C.I.D.S. that are hard to read, matter a lot, and can't be hedged: *Should I wed, commit, contract, hang out with, subscribe to, invest in, join into, participate with, cooperate on, belong to, believe in . . . ?*

Your questions are fundamentally the same ones that a cell must answer when choosing which molecules to let in. Neither you nor the cell can afford to affiliate with many dangerous things, nor can you afford to pass up affiliation with many sustaining things.

You both have to guess right. If you bet wrong too often, you die. And you both are wonderfully endowed with tools and guidance that enable you to get it right often enough to have earned the opportunity to live today.

Where you differ from the cell most is the number of different kinds of affinities you have to wonder about. A cell must be a master gatekeeper to molecules. You also play border guard to the molecules in your environment and food, but in addition you have to wonder which people, places, ideas, habits, products, activities, investments, and organizations to let in.

Why so choosy about your affiliations? It's this business about the sphere of influence. What you connect with influences you, changing your behavior. It actually filters you, amplifying some aspects of you and diminishing other aspects. Spend time with someone who frowns when you giggle and smiles when you're serious and that person filters your behavior, either making you more serious and less giggly if you are deferential, or more giggly and less serious if you're defiant. Either way, your behavior is influenced by coming into this person's orbit. We are each other's filters.

Therefore choose your influences wisely, investing time in healthy associations, efforts, and projects. And what does wisely mean? It means employing well that trial-and-error accumulation of adaptations you and your kind have been collecting for billions of years and still collect as you continue to learn from experience.

And it's not just a matter of choosing associates well. Investments of any kind filter you. Ideas you subscribe to filter your behavior and influence how you integrate subsequent ideas. The order in which you receive information matters since a previous idea changes your response to a subsequent one. A person who is exposed to his lifetime supply of bad news in childhood—exposed to atrocities of war and death, for example— is likelier to suffer depression than a person who gets an equal amount of bad news distributed evenly over a whole lifetime.

Not that we get to choose what we are exposed to always, or even often, especially in childhood. The stacking order of our affiliations is far from completely under our control. Still, most often when we do wonder what to do, it is often a question of selective affiliation. A big new investment of time, resources, and energy—will it be worth it?

Join vs. Don't Join

How it comes up:

> If Cue X, then join.
>
> If Cue Y, then don't join.

Getting it wrong:

False positive: Joining when you shouldn't.

False negative: Not joining when you should.

Too sure: Not doubting whether to join when doubting would have been useful.

Too unsure: Doubting whether to join when doubt wasn't useful.

Whirrings at Night:

Is this the career break I've been looking for?

Should I invest in that asset?

Am I going to regret moving in with them?

Will that machine pay for itself in more productivity?

Will this car turn out to be a lemon?

Why don't I feel like supporting them?

Why do I keep eating what I shouldn't?

Why do I keep falling in love with the wrong type?

Why didn't I pay attention when I still had a chance to pull out?

What they'll call you, if you:

	Don't Join	Join
Prove Right	Discerning	Decisive
	Energy-conserving	Bold
	Careful	Adventurous
Prove Wrong	Scared	Impulsive
	Stingy	Desperate
	Close-minded	Gullible

Just fork-edit:

'Become one with everything'
'Be Independent'

Here's a simple one-size-fits-all solution to the first wondering that you've surely heard:

Just let go. Always unite. End your greed and selfishness. Don't let your ego decide. United we stand, divided we fall. Befriend everyone and everything. Love even your enemy. Don't separate yourself. Be open. Barriers are unnatural. Stop blinding yourself to the real story—we are all one. What's wrong with this world is that people don't care enough, they push each other away. We should all just stop doing that.

Appealing in theory, stupid in practice—ask any immune system. Unite with the wrong thing and you're dead. Why then if it's stupid, do so many people find such platitudes appealing?

Doubt, when it's upon you, can be so taxing. It grabs your head in its big maw and shakes. It drains your spirit. The mysteries of life are great and all that, but when we're cornered with a high-stakes decision and are mystified as to what to do, we wish the mysteries would just leave us alone. Our ears perk up when an emancipating solution wafts by, even a stupid one, if it promises us eternal peace of mind.

As long as there's an appetite to find solutions to end all doubt, there will be guides, gurus, and consultants to recommend that we always just merge once and for all. Their version of things is most credible at small retreats at beautiful off-site locations where what goes around really comes around quickly and where acting nice and sweet to each other really pays off. If you haven't had a vacation from doubt into unity with all, you missed the counterculture and you missed something truly sweet. If you are invited to enjoy a mini-unity break, accept and enjoy, like a vacation into an imaginary land. You needn't worry too much about whether or not to take the advice to merge with everything too literally. You couldn't if you tried. So little time; so many possibilities for affiliation. Once you've decided to love humankind, you are forever burdened with the question, how much?

There are also teachers who acknowledge that sometimes you should and sometimes you shouldn't merge and that you need good guidance as to when to do which who will tell you about some exulted transcendental state you can reach in which all your *yes*'s and *no*'s will be the right ones. They allude to legendary masters who got a 100% on all gatekeeping tests because they had a system that you could have too. It involves becoming aware of everything—infinite attention, or at least infinite clarity about what to attend to.

And what is the system? Here the gurus get vague. Some talk about the easy calls at the extremes (You wouldn't want to be open to murders or closed to loved ones), but they don't give you much that you can apply to the tough judgment calls that keep you up at night. Like your older brother, they'll tell you that you wouldn't understand the system anyway unless you've reached it. It's amazing how many people invest in trying to reach this state given how few even the gurus admit have ever attained it.

The attractiveness of the system is not evidence of its utility but rather of our understandably insatiable appetite for ways to improve our adaptive toolkit for dealing with the wonders. Even empty promises of nonexistent systems sound better than ambiguity.

So, this teacher who promises new tools—is he or she worth learning from? The question itself is a wondering of the first kind—whether to adopt or reject an affiliation that's on offer. The answer is that it depends, but it should depend more on what the teacher supplies than on what you desire.

Take It Personally (T.I.P.)

The Guru's popularity is not primarily testament to his or her wisdom, but to our appetite for it.

Recognizing our insatiable appetite for good guidance will help us curb it a bit. Appreciating why we harbor romantic illusions of finding surefire ways out of doubt enables us to judge the guidance we're offered on its merit not its hype. The Guru beckons. You are curious but not desperate. You become a more discerning shopper.

Whatever else the spiritual quest is, it is certainly in part a human manifestation of life's incessant craving for better guidance about what to do. The high we feel in the presence of a "higher" consciousness must be in part excitement and anticipation at the prospect that we have finally found a definitive source of wisdom that we can tap and rely upon when choosing what to do that will free us from doubt. Spiritual or religious fervor, or even the enthusiasm we feel with a new coach, strategic consultant, therapist, self-help method, or philosophy is a testament to the strength of our craving to know what to do, and therefore not necessarily to the utility of the guidance on offer. Know this and you can prevent yourself from investing time, enthusiasm, and money in affiliations that will not pan out.

The Second Wondering of the Ancient World:

Should I Stick With This?

The second wondering naturally follows from the first: Once you have joined, affiliated with or committed to something, the wondering becomes whether to persist with it or shift. So instead of *Is it for me?* and *Should I invest?* we wonder, *Is it still for me?* or *Should I keep investing? Should I keep trying to make this marriage work? Am I kidding myself to think this business is ever going to be profitable? Is this kid ever going to straighten up? Will I ever get good at this or am I kidding myself?*

Oil wells come in three flavors: dry holes, gushers, and leakers. Dry holes and gushers are easy. Enjoy the gusher; walk away from the dry holes. Leakers keep the engineers guessing. Will it turn into a gusher or be a dry hole? Unless and until it does, they can't tell. The only thing worse than spending more on a dry hole is pulling out just before it becomes a gusher.

Thinking long and hard about the pros and cons of drilling deeper into any investment is a human-only activity, because we alone have an elaborate enough mind's eye screen upon which to parade out the evidence pro and con. Still, this wondering has been an issue for evolution to contend with ever since the first appearance of Lax and Ox—that which wants to try new things and that which wants to keep things the same. Evolution, wondering by genetic trial –and error, has always been a mix of shifting and persisting, mounting explorations for new solutions and exploiting found ones, retaining some things while varying others; trying to distinguish baby from bath water. You could call the evolutionary trial and error process by which we accumulate adaptations our re-creational vehicle not just because it re-creates us every day, but because it does so through this antagonism between R-Retention and V-Variation.

Genes change plans sometimes. How often? Just often enough to keep life going—not too much and not too little. How? In creatures that reproduce by cloning, through mutation; in sexual creatures, through cloning and recombination. When the rate of change that genetic mutation provided wasn't enough to keep up with fast changing environments, recombination became advantageous for many species, and all of the tools for guiding sexual behavior began to pass through Mother Nature's sieve. Through recombination—the shuffling together of two successful creatures' gene pools (like the deal making at invite-only networking events)—more variety was added.

When dealing with fundamental tensions you can get too much of two different good things. Too much variation is as dangerous as too little. Organic life is not likely to form on highly radioactive planets because radiation causes mutation to change things too rapidly. Too much change and life can't keep its adaptive toolkit together. Too little change and the toolkit can't keep up with changing circumstances.

The tension between sticking with things and changing them also plays out in other living creatures not just in their genetic processes but in their behavior as well. Sea bass typically mate for life, but change sexes regularly, swapping male and female roles. If the gender swapping gets uneven, imposing an unfair burden on one member of the pair, that member leaves. How does she (he) know when to back out of a bad deal? Evolution has granted her (him) the wisdom to know how to handle that tough judgment call.

Which just goes to show, when you're stuck in a rut and a fast changing world is passing you by, it's good to get out and mix it up with others, exchange ideas, and expose yourself to new possibilities. Lately with our business and technical environment changing so fast, the celebration of variation and change as opposed to tradition has reached ridiculous proportions. Change is good; stasis is bad. Well, it may take that much of an absolutist pep talk to get people out of their ruts, but if you take the rhetoric literally it ignores the necessary balance between change and stability. You can't think outside the box if you don't have one. To have a box that lasts you need to concentrate on the important question, which is not whether change is a good or a bad thing, but rather what should you change and what should you keep the same. What's a rut and what's a groove? Change all the time and you run the risk of being too open to get any work done. You lose your groove.

The power of words: A rut and a groove both describe retention. A groove is retention when you welcome it. A rut is

75

retention when you are praying for a little variation. The second wondering is whether it's a rut or a groove. You'd like to feel cocksure that it's a groove. Maybe you did once but now you're not sure. The groove isn't turning out the way you expected. You thought it would be a gusher and it isn't yet. Dry hole? Gusher? Dry hole? Gusher? Ooops. Now look, you're ping-ponging. How did you get there?

Maybe it's as simple as a single word. You were busy asking yourself, "How can I make this more of a groove?" Everything you've tried hasn't worked. Then one day you dropped the word "How" and asked simply, "Can I make this more of a groove?" and thereby opened yourself to the possibility that you're in a rut plain and simple. You were cocksure that it was a groove in need of repair, but now you're wondering whether it even has the potential of being a groove again. You are in limbo between cocksure and ping-pong wondering what to make of your doubt. Not sure, not even sure you are sure enough to keep trying to make it a groove.

The second wondering is especially hard on us humans because of that new tool of ours: the *I*, as in "I believe," "I'm committed," and "I've decided." The *I* is our flywheel—a great source of momentum, it's a sandbag we can plop down on top of any commitment we make to keep it from blowing away. It keeps us keeping on, but it can be hard to turn off when it's time to change course. For people with a very solid self-identity, the "I" is like a big thumb shifting the R-V balance in favor of retention. Knowing yourself with too much certainty can make you as steadfast and resistant to change as a cloning species, rolling out the same cookie-cutter choices day after day. Which is not necessarily a bad thing, as we'll see with the third wondering.

Having a less developed sense of self, a cat can change his mind more easily. No wonder we sometimes wish we had a cat's self-confidence, or lack of self-consciousness or both. The simplicity of a cat's choices makes them enviable.

Hold vs. Fold

How it comes up:

If cue X, then hold.

If cue Y, then fold.

Getting it wrong:

False positive: Holding when you should fold.

False negative: Folding when you should hold.

Too sure: Not doubting when doubting would be useful.

Too unsure: Doubting when doubt isn't useful.

Whirring at night:

Will my business ever become profitable?
Can this marriage be saved?
This shouldn't hurt this much.
I'm must not be cut out for this career.
I can't afford this doubt. I've got to have faith.
I'm no quitter; but I'm no fool either.
I have faith. This has got to work.

What they'll call you, if you:

	Fold	Hold
Prove **Right**	Disciplined	Dedicated
	Knows when to say enough	Loyal
		Persistent
Prove **Wrong**	Weak-willed	Stubborn
	Wishy-washy	Addicted
	Scared	In a rut

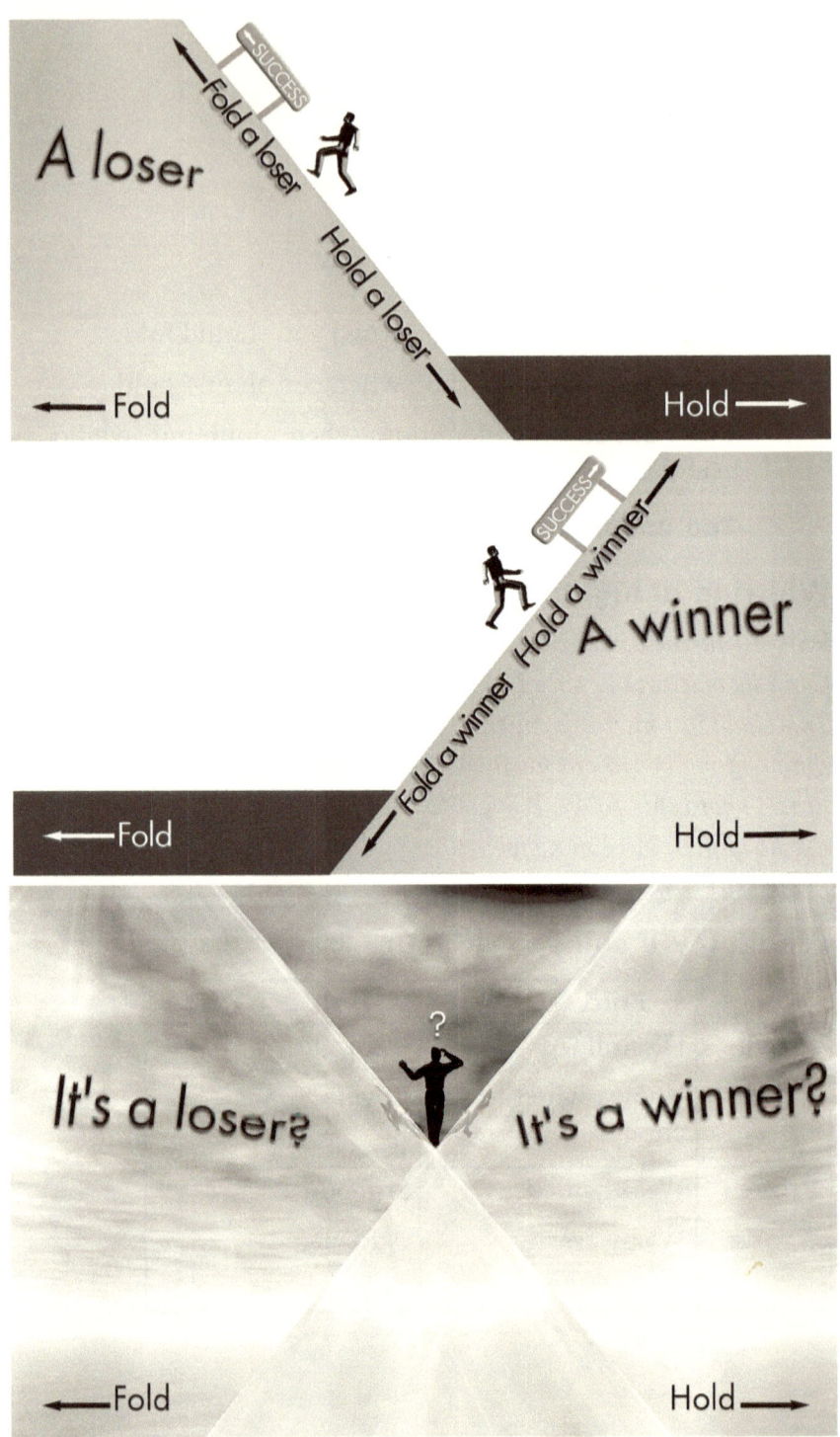

Just fork-edit:

'Persistence Furthers'

'Enough's enough'

As with the first wondering, there are simple, appealing, but wrong absolute solutions to the second.

Always persist. Persistence furthers; when the going gets tough, the tough get going; it's always darkest before the dawn. Never say die. Never? Of course not. Sometimes it's darkest before death, and to avoid it you have to paddle like hell in a new direction. Think of the Jews who changed plans and left Nazi Germany before it was too late. Would persistence in the Germany of the 1930s have furthered?

If only it were as simple as "Always persist." Then we'd always know what to do—like in the movies, the dogged hero persisting and then prevailing against all odds, teaching us over and over the simple but inaccurate lesson that we should always do what we've resolved to do.

Why do so many people believe that persistence always furthers if it doesn't? Why do we want to be told that it does almost every time we take in a picture show?

The answer resides in the *I* again, the uniquely human way we pin ourselves down by identifying personally with our commitments. Marrying ourselves to our commitments strengthens these commitments; it makes us capable of long-term investments that no animal could make. The history of culture can be seen as an increasingly widespread need to muster self-discipline to pull off increasingly long-term, high-stakes investments in increasingly complex projects. In the old days, workers did not rely on self-discipline so much, more on self-preservation. The Pharaoh told the builders what to do. The builders knew their place and deferred, with the exception eventually of Moses' tribe. Indeed Moses sets an early example of the kind of self-determination that has created the vacuum that must now be filled with self-motivation. To be your own boss requires that you filter your own behavior and that takes discipline.

Hold vs. Fold

Self-determination has been good for us. It has produced the variety of human achievements and disciplines now open to self-determining people. A teen today faces a blizzard of options and does so without a credible Pharaoh to make the choice for her. "Should I stay invested?" becomes an increasingly pressing question.

Our world has become a more complex place. Fewer good things come easy; success takes greater commitment, more sandbags; and there is a higher cost to moving on and a greater temptation to anticipate failure, so we need encouragement.

A strong sense of self serves us going into a project and persisting, but it does so at a price paid later if the project doesn't pay off. By anteing up your Self on a project, you motivate yourself to make the project work but run the risk of being devastated if it doesn't. The self is held hostage to the project's success.

No pain, no gain can be misconstrued as an argument that feeling pain means you should persist. But pain means no such thing. Even though most gain does require persistence through hardship, not all persistence through hardship leads to gain.

Therefore, if anything is going to worry you, it's hints that you've bet wrong, which come easily these days on big projects even if you haven't. We get a little hair-trigger at times, ready to bolt when the going gets tough. Therapists sometimes attribute a client's failure to complete projects to "fear of success." If there is such a thing it probably doesn't upstage fear of failure in our mind's eye horror movies. A habit of not finishing things is more plausibly attributable to the universal human reaction to the high-stakes investments we humans are uniquely capable of making. There's only so much anticipation of losing on high-stakes gambits that we can stand before we bail out just to get some stress-relief. The movies help us compensate for this tendency to bolt, by showing us people who didn't bolt and as a result became superheroes.

The "no-pain-no-gain" Protestant work ethic became a solid argument for persistence at arduous tasks around the time that self-determination, options, and project size were increasing. At the time when people started doing bigger, more abstract things not out of necessity, the work ethic may have had as strong an appeal as the "change everything" work ethic has had in the

80

"new economy." The most expedient way to counterbalance one absolute is with its opposite. To compensate for a tendency to bail out prematurely, we say "always persist" and watch movie after movie in which it proves to have been the right thing to do. Similarly, the celebration of change discussed previously offsets a tendency to stick with the traditional that was proving increasing inappropriate in our accelerating world: Tradition is always good? Absolutely not. Change is always good. It's not true but it is sometimes strategically useful to overcompensate, like when you notice that you drew the bath too cold, turning the hot on full blast. It does compensate but if you ignore the bath for a while you can end up with a bath that is too hot. So it's good to remember the balance between the two antagonistic forces is what you want, not rash oscillations between them. The Sufis have a saying that captures the ping-ponging between absolutes perfectly: "He who is burnt by hot milk blows on ice cream."

People learn from past mistakes. That's part of the adaptive process. Still watch out not to learn too fast.

Just because you burnt yourself working on something that didn't pan out, it doesn't mean the next bet will go south too. And just because a movie hero persisted and won doesn't mean you will. Remember that a screenwriter can work backward from a final scene, whereas you can't. As Danish philosopher Soren Kierkegaard said, "Life can only be understood backwards . . . but must be lived forwards." You don't know what is going come of your investments. You have to decide when to quit and when to persist.

Take It Personally (T.I.P.)

Even when you bet right it still can come out wrong.

Pick a card, any card, but before you do, which you prefer—one hundred dollars if it's a face card or one hundred dollars if it's a number card? There are 40 number cards and 12 face cards. Number cards are a better bet so that's the bet you place. You pick a card and it's the king of hearts.

Did you bet wrong? Of course not. Betting right and coming out right are two different things. The only time they're the same is when it's not a bet but a certainty.

Remember a bet you placed that came out wrong, one in which you stuck with some investment longer than you should have? Do you tell the story that it was a bad bet or a good bet that came out badly? If you call it a bad bet, you probably hope not to place bets like that again. What features of the bet did you conclude were the warning signs that you wish you had heeded and vow to heed now so you don't make that kind of bad bet again? Can you think of a situation in which a bet would be worth making even if those warning signs were present? That is, a situation in which you could bet wrong and it could turn out right after all?

It's a wiggly world. Good bets come out bad; bad bets come out good. And these surprise outcomes do not free you from placing bets or living with doubt about the bets you place, because educated bets are better than random ones—more often than not. You never can tell what will come of your bets, and though some people give fatalistic lip service to this as an argument against betting carefully, it has never kept anyone from trying to place good bets. You can't know absolutely, and yet some bets are better than others.

The Third Wondering of the Ancient World:

Should I Be Consistent Here?

The third wondering is whether to hold a behavior constant or alter it with different circumstances.

Toggling—doing different things in different situations is life's best response to dilemmas. Remember our *if/then* statements? Toggles, that's what they are. In situation X, go with plan A. In situation Y go with plan B. When we were looking at them before, we just posited them for illustrative purposes. But really, where do they come from? They are adaptations. They are the wisdom that accumulates through life's trial-and-error processes and they are the main way that life deals with dilemmas.

It's the obvious solution. If there are trade-offs—costs and benefits to plans A and B—why not do each in the situations that will yield the most benefits and least costs from each plan? Toggle over time (Plan A today, plan B tomorrow) and over space (Plan A in the presence of X, Plan B in the presence of Y). Nothing could be more basic. In the ever-popular serenity prayer (which is the fourth wondering of the ancient world, by the way. Coming up.) we ask for the courage to change what we can and the serenity to accept what we can't and *the wisdom to know the difference.* That's toggling, pure and simple, and whenever you've got the right wisdom, you've solved your dilemmas as well as they can be solved, placing the optimal bets. If your wisdom works well enough, it can even work automatically, making decisions for you while you sleep silently and glitch-free.

We have a great many wise toggles embodied already. Biologists originally thought genes possessed complete blueprints for specific traits, one per gene predetermined at inception to give you either blue eyes or brown eyes. They are much more complex than that, it turns out, with cascades of interacting toggles with genes that produce proteins that switch other proteins on and off under different situations.

Organisms themselves are never one-trick ponies either. A microscopic relative of lobsters called Daphnia makes offspring with or without hardened shells depending on whether the mother's body detects the presence of predators in her water environment. The hard shell has its costs and benefits. It takes energy to produce so it's only worth it if the predator is around. If (predator) then (make shell). If (no predator) then (save energy). The best of both worlds.

Consistency vs. Flexibility

A warm-blooded animal maintains a constant body temperature by toggling his metabolism; a cold-blooded animal maintains a constant metabolism with a shifting body temperature. When in danger, a mammal toggles from parasympathetic to sympathetic nervous response, turning off very useful functions that use energy that under the circumstances is better spent getting out of danger. If (no danger) then (digest). If danger then (save energy). When the threat is gone, the mammal's body shifts back to the parasympathetic response.

Sensible toggling is a characteristic of all life. It's a masterful way of dealing with the fundamental dilemmas in life. Should you do A or B? Why not do A when it will work best and B when it will? Toggling is how one hedges bets when one can. Toggling is how life responds to a wondering with "It depends."

So toggle everything? No. Toggling itself is expensive. It requires switching mechanisms and creates more complexity. The greatest cost of toggling is toggling wrong—switching to plan A when B is better or vice versa. When your commitment to plan A is working out well enough, why try to improve upon it by shifting between A and B with good timing?

Toggling is how we bet. The two most common bets are affiliate or don't affiliate (the two solutions debated in the first and second wonderings we've just discussed). So here's an example of a situation in which toggling isn't worth it: Consider two alternative approaches to the stock market. One is buying stocks and holding them; the other is toggling in and out of the market—holding or folding, entering or exiting the market depending on whether stocks are likely to go up or down. In principle, toggling out on the downturn, and in on the upturn sounds like a great approach, but getting it wrong is worse than just staying in. A toggling or timing investor who bet wrong on the five best days between 1970 and 1994 would make half as much a someone who didn't toggle but kept money in throughout.

So how much toggling is the right amount? Between the maximum and the minimum. What should you keep constant and what should you toggle? Between everything and nothing. Often a single toggling element is enough to keep a system in equilibrium. For example, to keep your home at a constant temperature, you don't need to toggle the windows, doors, and shades open and closed, to change the pitch of your roof, and the thickness of the walls. All you need is one toggle—the thermostat switching on and off the heater.

Firm vs. Flexible

How it comes up:

If cue X, then do plan A.

If cue Y then if cue Z then do plan B, otherwise do plan A.

Getting it wrong:

False positive: Being consistent when you should toggle.

False negative: Toggling when you should be consistent.

Too sure: Not doubting when doubting would be useful.

Too unsure: Doubting when doubt isn't useful.

Whirring at Night:

I'd love having a boyfriend again but I'm so enjoying living alone. Maybe I should get over it and move him in, or maybe I can keep him but not have him live here.

I should never have pushed my daughter so hard. Or maybe pushing her was right before but not now. She's going through a phase and it's time for me to back off for a while.

What they'll call you, if you:

	Be Consistent	**Toggle**
Prove	Steady	Attentive
Right	Reliable	Accommodating
	Dependable	Flexible
Prove	Mechanical	Mercurial
Wrong	Predictable	Inconsistent
	Stodgy	Vacillating

Consistency vs. Flexibility

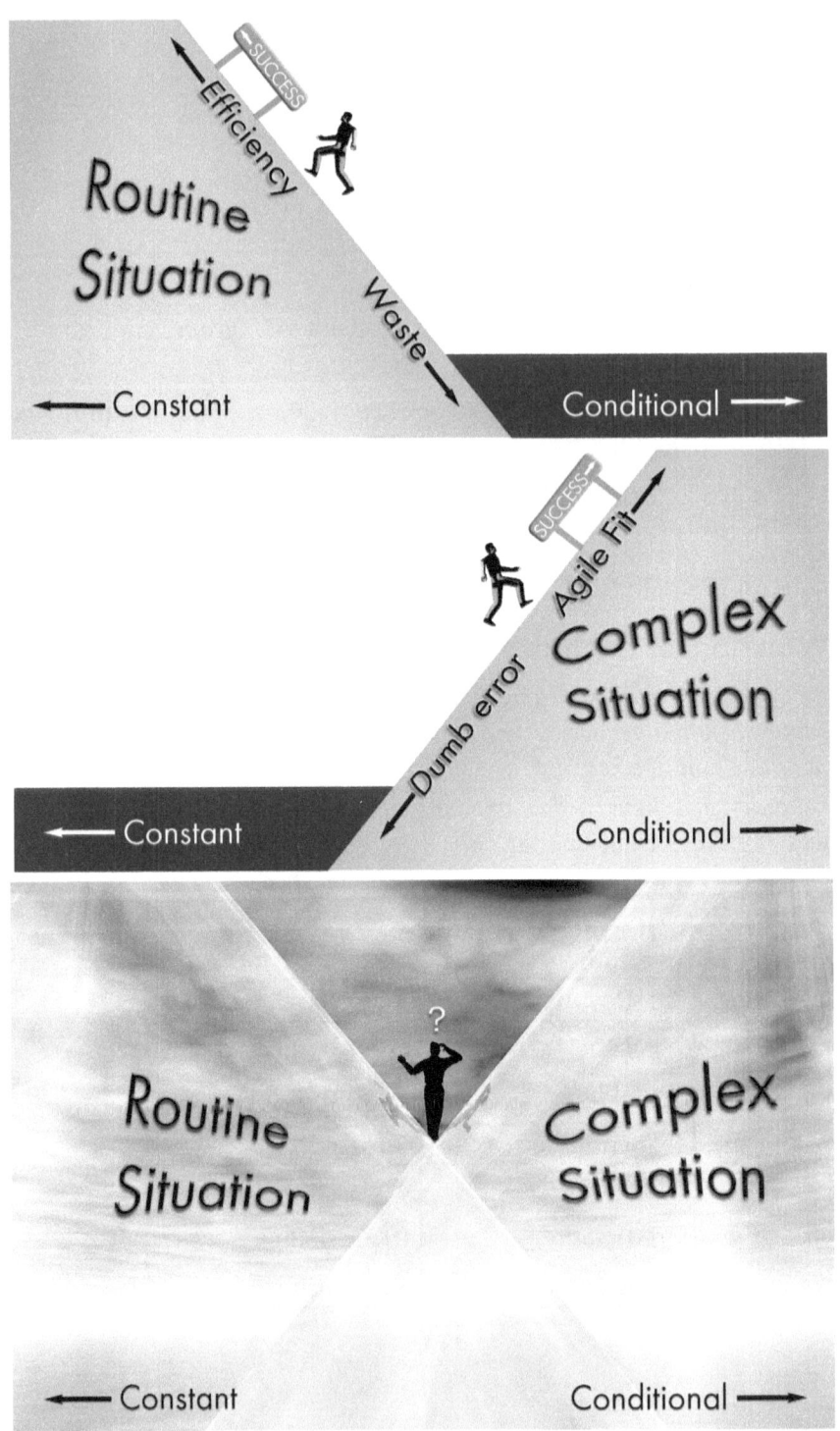

Just fork-edit:

'Always be constant'
'Always be flexible'

Traditionalists and reformers square off with absolutes like these. But no one can be always constant or always flexible. Intrinsic to the design of this world is a fundamental shortage on both constancy and flexibility. Remember the freelancer considering whether to return to salaried work? We'd all like perfect freedom to do what feels most appropriate to the circumstances and perfect constancy from our environment so that whatever feels most appropriate is available the moment we want it. Few of us demand such an unreasonable expectation outright, but none of us would turn it down if we were offered it. And indirectly we imply this wish in conversation, especially in heated conversation or negotiation between two people over who gets to do what. People who would prefer that you were more constant with them are the greatest advocates of constancy as a virtue. People who would prefer that you gave them more flexibility to follow their whims are the greatest advocates of freedom as an absolute virtue.

For you to have the option to come and go as you please and still find your options waiting when you return requires that the sources of your options remain constant. Thus, collectively we demand more constancy from each other than we can supply and therefore more freedom than any of us can afford without imposing upon each other.

In our youth we tried toggle-free love, the full commitment to constancy. Do you remember, perhaps in high school, rushing into joined-at-the-hip-forever devotion and the sense that you would keep it up as long as forever, the way they do in the songs? A figment of complete satisfaction, it lasted a while and thrilled us until it fizzled. Adjusting to this reality we learned to toggle, not throwing ourselves all the way into it but saving a little bit of ourselves for ourselves. Ever since then, we've had to negotiate with our partners over commitment and freedom—how much and when. It takes more effort to negotiate satisfying relationships between two people who toggle than between two people who single-mindedly commit. But it's worth it. Think of a kingdom with matching harem that it would take to give just one person complete freedom to follow whims in love; think of the constancy exacted from the concubines. It's not a scheme you can roll out for mass consumption.

Where constancy as a virtue is most absolute and where these days the shortage is becoming the biggest problem is with children. They need constancy and these days there's not enough of it to go around. Parents are distracted. There are many possible explanations but one that gets overlooked is an unusual evolutionary one.

The usual evolutionary interpretation of human parenting is that couples bond with each other and with their children in order to provide them with a healthy start. The instinct to do so is exactly the kind of adaptation you'd expect in creatures like us. It's exactly the kind of hard wiring that would make it so our adaptations would continue to pass successfully generation after generation through Mother Nature's sieve. Mothers, the conventional wisdom goes, are hard wired to be constant with children more than fathers are because they have all the hormones and bodily changes of childbirth that keep them committed.

The unconventional evolutionary story is about what is now competing with both parents' constancy. Today, children compete with brainchildren for their parents' attention. It happened with act three of our natural history of doubt. Before act three the only thing that mattered the only ultimate determinant of what lived and what died was success at passing through Mother Nature's sieve, which takes making children. But in act three, when we became mental movie makers a new ultimate determinant came into play and took on a life of its own. Our mental movies are our brainchildren and getting them through our cultural sieve has taken on a life of its own. Parents are distracted with getting their brainchildren off to a good start. Brainchildren? How many of us get to invent ideas from scratch? Well, how many of us get to make children from scratch? Remember, as Kahil Gibran put it, your children are "the sons and daughters of Life's longing for itself." You didn't make their genes, you mixed and matched them and passed them on. Similarly, in the Brainchild Age, you mix and match mental movies and pass them on. The traveling salesperson is spreading the company's brainchildren. Teachers, scientists, engineers, chefs, doctors, carpenters—these days we all buy, sell, or use tools, modern day adaptations built from ideas and wisdom for getting things done. The brainchild economy grows and filters wisdom faster than evolution ever has before which makes the exploding brainchild economy attractive and distracting.

Especially because the mixing and matching is happening at a furiously fascinating pace. The recombination that happens with brainchildren is fluid. It IS in fact the deal making that happens at invite-only networking events, not in the sense that only the invitees are making the deals, but rather that ideas themselves are invite-only. They are the ideas that have passed through culture's sieve. Successful technologies recombine to beget other successful technologies. We are enjoying a brainchild population explosion.

Enjoying and suffering it. Today some women suffer from what could be called "Midwife Crisis." Midway through the time they thought they would be married and raising children. they remember what it was they were about to do when their biological clock woke them up with the biochemistry of baby making. In their teens they were into the brainchild economy but got diverted by the age-old embodied wisdom "make kids," which coursed through their bodies making decisions for them, decisions leading to family and marriage. When the kids get older, the biochemical bath drains out and the wife looks around, wondering what happened, how she got shanghaied into spending all day at home with the kids, and how she can "midwife" herself back into the brainchild economy where she belongs. She leaves like the put-upon sea bass whose mate plays the man one time too many.

The likeliest culprit is Dad, who also distracted by the brainchild evolution came to rely upon Mom's biochemically subsidized commitment to family as an opportunity to go out and make a career, not ever expecting that the subsidy would wear off as the kids got older. Both the wife's resentment and the husband's behavior are understandable, but only if you understand the underlying trend. Most people don't, and so midwife crisis is often bloody, and the children suffer, exposed to inconstancy too soon.

Consistency vs. Flexibility

How soon is too soon to break the news to children that the world does not offer any of us an abundance of constancy? Answering this question is perhaps the greatest challenge a parent faces. Breaking that news too soon can make them unnecessarily fearful and depressed. Breaking it too late can make them spoiled or gullible, susceptible to a false sense of security.

The life of Buddha, according to legend, began with an inordinately long period of parental protectiveness. His father, a king, was determined that his son should become a great leader and not a spiritual teacher as had been prophesied. He made complex arrangements to protect his son from any evidence that life is hard and unpredictable. When Buddha, already a young adult, was suddenly exposed to death, aging, and disease, the startling revelation was enough to make him give up everything to study the nature of suffering. His life turned out well, which goes to show you never can tell how soon is too soon. Even the argument that exposing children to inconstancy is certain to produce traumatized children may not be constantly true. One of the other great challenges of child rearing is that every practice that succeeds for one child will not necessarily work for another.

During the child's young years he or she takes little steps away from Mom. Mom makes herself constantly available at first. The child takes longer steps away, until finally, no longer relying on Mom's constancy, he or she leaves home. Then it's the parent's turn to wish for more constancy, reminding the child of the virtue of it, and of calling more regularly. The grown child isn't fickle; but rather constant elsewhere. Only when our children grow up does it dawn on us that they pay us back by raising their children, the way we paid back our parents not directly but by raising the next generation.

Take it Personally (T.I.P.)

Attention is a pinhole in a flood.

A simple absolute like "Be constant" distracts us from the fact that being constant in one circumstance necessarily precludes being constant in another. You have finite energy and you can't be in two places at once. In economics the trade-off is called an "opportunity cost." If you buy one thing, the opportunity cost is doing without whatever you didn't buy instead.

When deciding where to selectively invest your constancy, keep the opportunity costs in mind. If you want to start being constant someplace new, make room for it. For example, don't imagine that you can fit every hobby that interests you into your schedule. Mastery requires constancy. Most of us, if we are good at anything at all, got that way by not following our every whim, but by instead investing constantly at one interest to the exclusion of others for more time than we cared to. In the brainchild population explosion the opportunity costs increase exponentially. There are so many more things you are foregoing these days, whatever it is you're focused on.

Life has always been about allocating finite attention in a world of infinite options. That's what wisdom is for. You can use an awareness of this to your advantage in helping you maintain or shift your focus. Notice that having reasons to NOT focus on things is important. Sometimes the best insights are "outsights"—ones that enable you to ignore things—putting them out of sight so you can focus elsewhere. If you want replace an old focus, upstage it with a new one. If you are trying to get over a lost love, remember that it's always harder to give up something for nothing. Find something new that rivets your finite attention because it will help you take your mind off the other.

The Fourth Wondering of the Ancient World:

Can I Improve This?

Life's biggest question is how to allocate finite energy in a world of infinite options. A creature isn't infinite. It can only do so much. So little energy, so many options. The wisdom to know which options to attend to and which options to ignore is the key to success.

But success by what standard? What constitutes a good allocation? For nonhuman creatures, any allocation that increases the chances that the organism's toolkit will pass through Mother Nature's sieve is a good one. With advances in biology over the past one hundred years we now know that biological reproductive success is what makes or breaks a family line and has made or broken them since the beginning. The traits and behaviors that accumulate in a family line's toolkits are those that enable an organism to allocate its finite energy to those options that serve directly or indirectly to increase its chance of making offspring that survive to make more offspring.

Beyond that, the only other rule is simple: Whatever works. Mother Nature holds no universal moral standards. As the sieve-holding gatekeeper, deciding which living lineages get to pass on their toolkits, Mother Nature is disturbingly tolerant. Now that biologists have gathered so many details about living things' personal lives, there's no getting around it. Morality is defined locally in each species. Baby Australian Social Spiders eat their mother and gestating siblings. In their world it's appropriate. Mother makes herself available by dissolving her pregnant body into a slurry of nutrients in time for her hatching eggs' first meal.

We can't hold spiders to the same moral standards as we hold for ourselves, but the fact that spiders live by different moral standards is no reason to hold our human morals any loosely. We are decidedly human and can't make excuses for eating relatives by citing the behavior of spiders.

Our morality is different from any other creatures. Culture, for mental movie-making creatures like us, is a public library of useful mental movie footage, gives us a new and powerful way to hold wisdom that guides us in our allocation of finite energy. Our culture's morals are embodied wisdom too, also accumulating by trial and error, and now an intrinsic component of the selection of things—natural selection, feeling selection, mental movie selection, cultural selection, etc.—that make up our minds.

While "whatever works," is all Mother Nature asks, we can make a few more generalizations about what her standards turn out to be. For example, in the service of making offspring, it's useful to invest one's finite energy in transforming options into more energy. It takes energy to get energy so that's where a lot of energy goes.

For example, almost all of us living creatures absorb sunlight directly or as food, which is stored sunlight. And a lot of our adaptations serve us by helping us find and make use of food that we can successfully transform into more energy. It's exactly like what businesses go through. It takes money to make money, and a lot of a business's energy must go into picking opportunities to spend money to bring in more money. Businesses and bodies go bankrupt when they run out of energy with which to go get more energy.

In this very broad sense therefore, one of life's perennial tough judgment calls is whether interacting with something will yield more energy or energy savings. It's as though every living thing's body must seek answers to the question, "Can I transform this into more energy, and/or energy savings?"

Think of it as one of the most universal toggling behaviors living systems need. Investing one's finite attention in some options and not others, we focus on what we can transform and what we can't.

If transformable, then attend to it, invest in it, use it.

If un-transformable, then ignore it.

We die when we get it wrong, investing in trying to transform what we can't transform, or ignoring the things that we can transform.

All of this is by way of saying that the fourth wondering of the ancient world is simply the Serenity Prayer that no doubt is already familiar to you:

"God, grant me the courage to change what I can, the serenity to accept what I can't and the wisdom to know the difference. . . ."

Christian philosopher Reinhold Niebhur wrote this as the opening line of a Christian prayer. In its entirety it evokes surrender, " . . . taking as Jesus did, this sinful world as it is, not as I would have it, trusting that You [God] will make all things right if I surrender to Your will."

The first part of the prayer is the only part that most people know. It rings resonantly for Christians and non-Christians alike. The Serenity Prayer is extremely popular because it encapsulates one of the most important wonderings of the world so succinctly.

What we pray for is the wisdom to know the difference between what can and can't be transformed. Who we pray to, if to anyone at all, is not the point. What is universal about the prayer is how we pray—by trial and error and always with a way to retain the wisdom—in genes, in culture, in physical memory of pleasure and pain, in cognitive memory, or in mental movie film footage. That, and the fact that the praying we do is a matter of life and death practicality and has been since the beginning.

Since the beginning, Mother Nature (who is not a person though it is useful to think of her as one) longing for herself, "prayed" for the wisdom, and ever since Mother Nature was able to embody wisdom in sentience, a creature's ability to feel pleasure and pain, living creatures themselves have longed for the wisdom to know the difference between what they could and couldn't transform, taking pleasure in transformation's consequences and suffering in its absence.

The term *adaptation* contains a double meaning; it can mean accommodate, adjust to, get use to—a kind of surrender to what is. The term *adaptation* in perceptual psychology means getting used to a signal—a smell or a sound, for example, if it continues for long enough. But adaptation also means a trait or behavior that enables a creature to actively transform its environment. A beaver can't transform the cold weather to good effect, so evolution equips it with a thick fur coat. It can transform trees into shelter, so evolution equips it with sharp teeth. All adaptations are tools that enable a living being to either ignore or accommodate to what can't change, or find and interact with what it can. The question then is when to do which. The last thing you want to do is try to change what you can't change or accept what you need not accept. Adaptations at their core then are embodied judgment calls about what is worth trying to change and what isn't.

A frog's brain registers only a few kinds of signals from its environment—little black fly spots flitting about, big shadows encroaching rapidly—just the minimum, the options and opportunities that the frog can transform into energy and energy savings. The rest it ignores. Why? Because in allocating its finite energy and attention a frog is best off ignoring what it cannot transform. The pebbles on the bank of the pond are un-transformable. Though they are always there, they do not enter the frog's awareness. The frog's faculty for attending to some and ignoring other signals is part of the frog's adaptive toolkit or "wisdom to know the difference" that has successfully passed through the particular sieve Mother Nature filters frog-tools through. Indeed, a frog sitting in a bucket of stunned flies will starve to death because the frog doesn't perceive the nutritional value in flies unless they're flitting. In a frog's natural environment—the sieve that Mother Nature has presented to frogs for millions of years—missing out on lifeless flies was not enough of a squandering of opportunity to prevent the frog's toolkit from passing through the sieve. A focus on flitting flies has worked well enough.

"Grant me the wisdom"—there's our healthy longing for better tools. It is often preceded by the word God. Whatever else God is, he, she, or it is certainly a symbol of higher authority. We would just love to discover that there is some higher authority we could go to who could tell us what is transformable and what isn't.

If you can't transform your well into a gusher, then pull out. If you can transform it, then keep digging. If you can't tell, you're left to wonder whether the courage to dig on or the serenity to pull out is the most appropriate response.

A lot more can be said about wondering what you can and can't change, particularly as it applies to what you can and can't change about other people and about yourself. It is such a significant wondering that it will reappear as the third wondering of the modern world applied specifically to what you can and can't change about your fellow humans and yourself.

Accept vs. Exert

How it comes up:

If it can't be changed to good effect, then accept.

If it can be changed to good effect, then exert.

Getting it wrong:

False positive: Courage to change what can't be changed.

False negative: Serenity to accept what could be changed.

Too sure: Not doubting whether you can change something when doubting would be useful.

Too unsure: Doubting whether you can change something when doubting is useful.

Whirrings at Night:

Is this as good as it gets?
There must be a better way. I hope . . .
Why am I taking this lying down?
Why do I have so much trouble accepting?
Why don't I have more gumption?
Why can't I accept things the way they are?
Is this my fate? Is it hard wired? God's will?

What they'll call you, if you:

	Guess changeable	Guess unchangeable
Prove Right	Realistic Honest Sober	Determined Courageous Undaunted
Prove Wrong	Pessimistic Impotent Wimpy	Fool-hardy A dreamer Too hopeful

Just fork-edit:

'You can change anything if you put your mind to it'
'Accept the world as it is'

"There's nothing you can't do if you put your mind to it. Therefore always maintain a can-do attitude. Think of Edison, Ford, Gandhi." We need to hear this. We lean close and open our ears wide, drinking deeply the song of triumph sung by the guy who changed something that the whole world thought couldn't be changed. Still, for every famously successful maverick, there are many un-famous mavericks who failed to change what they tried to, despite trying with all their might. So think of these failures too.

Here's the catch: You can't tell what's changeable until you try to change it. It's as though the universe holds back the full potential for changing something until you pony up your full commitment. Maybe that's reason enough to always commit. After all, the universe will lend support once you do. But how much support? Maybe a lot, maybe a little, but you can't tell in advance. How, therefore, can you assess your prospect of changing something until you've committed to changing it? And once you're committed it's often hard to un-commit if it proves not particularly changeable.

Call it "Guesscrow," a sort of catch-22 dilemma: The universe has some support for your prospective venture sitting in an escrow account awaiting your commitment. You can't find out how much support you'll get from the universe until you commit, and you don't want to commit until you have a good guess what's in the escrow account.

Think of how guesscrow affects people's love lives. You can't really know what potential there is to transform a date into a soul mate until you commit yourself. Choose love therefore, or so the story goes. But by choosing love you don't guarantee that you'll become soul mates. At most you release your full potential which may not be much. And if it's not much, then what? How loving is it to have declared yourself a person's soul mate and then pull back when your test-authentic commitment fails? What do you say when they cry, "I thought you said you loved me. Were you lying?"

"No. Trying."

It's dangerous to assume that the universe will back you in transforming things the way you want, but the people who believe it wil often gain an extra oomph of power charisma and gumption that takes their projects over the top into success.

When a problem persists against our usual repertoire of responses, we really have only two choices. One is to accept the problem as beyond our control. The other is to press on in the conviction that we can solve it. The reason that there are only two choices is that either works best when embraced to the exclusion of the other. Half-accepting frees up too little energy. Half a can-do attitude usually means you can't do after all. Life often beseeches us to make either-or decisions.

It would be great if we could hedge, both persisting in trying to transform a thing and at the same time giving up. That's the solution that seems most appropriate. But it's hard to hold the courage to change something and the serenity to accept it at the same time. The two attitudes erode each other. As soon as you doubt you can do something, you probably can't. As soon as you're sure you can do something, you reduce your chance of discovering a graceful exit if you turn out to be wrong. Recognizing that the middle ground is ineffectual, we use our stories, analogies, absolutist declarations, and fork-edits like oars to paddle ourselves to a pole at either end of the continuum between can-do and can't. These baldly absolutist declarations are our either-oars.

To save a marriage, tell stories of divorce as failure, incompatibilities as minor, persistence as virtue, marriage as sacred. To accept the marriage as over, tell stories of transformation as enriching, change as inevitable, divorce as liberation.

Our either-oar stories move us across the sea of ambiguity and out toward the poles. But sometimes we change our minds. Our either-oars get shot full of holes by evidence, and we carve ourselves a new pair to paddle as quickly as we can toward the opposite pole.

In this sense we are all spin doctors. The absolutes—you can change anything or nothing—are useful either-oars, not because they are true but because they help us paddle ourselves toward the cocksureness necessary to extract as much reward from our bets as we possibly can. Once we've made a decision either to try to change something or to accept it as is, we spin it convincingly for ourselves and others. Either-oars help us paddle away from foregone options when they are most persistently encroaching upon our commitments and eroding our resolve.

There are plenty of reasons to use spin to affirm decisions, but spin is best when it knows its place. Spin is best suited for decision-affirmation, not decision making. In decision making, you want an open mind about the ambiguity of the real choices you face. Therefore, try to notice when you're spinning and when you aren't. Try to notice the spin other people try to sell you on too. Don't let decision-affirming strategies make your decisions for you. Sometimes you can change things and sometimes you can't.

Take It Personally (T.I.P.)

Turn off the spin when you are deciding. Turn on the spin when you've already decided.

Think of it as The Spin doctor's Hippocratic Oath: To reinforce a decision you've already made, turn on the power of positive (can-do) and negative (can't do) thinking. But when you are making a decision, cultivate the power of neutral (maybe can; maybe can't) thinking.

A good way to explore options when making a decision is to try a number of different spins to see which fits. Ping-ponging as described earlier, is like trying on the pros and cons as though you meant them. One could try saying, "I can't just quit my job," and alternatively, "I've just got to get out of this dead-end job," and see which of the two rings truer and fits better. To really try them, say them as though you mean them. But beware. If in testing an idea you say it too convincingly you run the risk of forgetting that you are just testing it. This is like walking into a clothes store, trying on a pair of pants, and deciding that you must own them since you've already got them on you. Why would people make this mistake? Indecision isn't fun and there are a lot of social pressures to act decisively. The temptation is great to get over it and move on—to jump straight from ping-pong to cocksure ASAP.

And often it's not a mistake at all. Making time for doubt is useful only for certain decision making. Most of the time, taking the first option that comes to mind and fits is perfectly adequate. The catch is that it is often hard to tell which decisions would benefit from thought and doubtfulness and which ones wouldn't, and because of the eagerness most of us feel to get over doubt the Spin Doctor's Hippocratic Oath helps counteract a tendency to move too hastily toward cocksureness.

To apply the Spin doctor's Hippocratic oath requires the ability to keep track of when you are deciding and when you have decided. Know the difference between "try," and "buy." When trying, be neutral or ping-pong gingerly. But once you've placed your bet, be able to turn on the spin because it gives you power to persuade yourself and others, the power to unleash whatever energy the Universe is going to allocate in support of your decision.

Accept vs. Exert

A good way to make sure you don't walk off with the wrong pants is to carry a few pairs of pants into the dressing room. That way you don't forget that you have options. Likewise a good way to make sure you don't walk off with the wrong decision is to bring a few options into the decision-making process. Throwing your full weight into two or three divergent options at the beginning of a decision-making process can be a great way to limber up, and if you are making a group decision, it's a great way to make clear that you're are still making a decision rather than just converging on group-think.

The Fifth Wondering of the Ancient World:

Is This A Cue?

Should you invest or not? Should you stay invested or not? Should you toggle or not? Can you transform this thing or not? The answer to the first four wonderings of the ancient world is: It depends.

On what? That's the fifth wondering: What cues will tip you off on which way to bet?

All living beings respond to their environments, changing behavior in response to conditions. There are no one-trick ponies. There aren't even one-trick plankton. Responsiveness requires perception—the ability to detect cues in one's environment—or else there's nothing to respond to.

Cue-reading tools are crucial and if you get the wrong ones—responding to the wrong cues or ignoring the right ones, you are in trouble. So little energy, so many potential cues. Life wonders which cues matter.

A snake's forked tongue detects scents in stereo. If the left fork scents more hot flesh than the right fork, the snake moves leftward. The faintest mist of meat has proven a useful cue, in particular if it is stronger on one side of its forked tongue than on the other.

E. coli bacteria have two modes of swimming: straight ahead and random tumbling. A bacterium swims straight unless it drifts to where there's nothing to eat and then it tumbles, hopefully onto a changed course to the sugar it needs. How does it know that there's nothing to eat? A sugar-cue tool.

And you? Copious cues, some of which you take for granted. Wavelengths on the electromagnetic spectrum range from less than one billionth of a meter to a thousand meters, yet without instruments we humans can only perceive the tiniest sliver of that range—between 400 and 700 billionths of a meter—a range which happens to correspond to things worth noticing for creatures like us—green things to eat and solid stuff to avoid bumping into. Your visual obsession with the subtle differences in the tiniest little band of the electromagnetic spectrum is an adaptive keeper, a cue-detection tool that has passed through Mother Nature's sifter because it helps you distinguish between the ripe and unripe fruit that you can and can't transform into nutrients and now enabling you to distinguish between what can and can't transform you— the invisible air you can pass through and that solid-looking rock that will transform your nose if you bump into it.

Three and a half billion years is a long time to be acquiring and refining our list of cues to attend to. You'd think that maybe by now we'd have it down pat, knowing what to heed and what to ignore in order to make good choices. Although we've come a long way, we're not done and never will be:

First, with finite attention we can't attend to every cue that possibly matters, candidate cues compete for our very limited attention. Second, incumbent cues that used to matter don't necessarily matter any more. For example, many of us well past our parental prime still obsess over physical cues that signal a potential mate's fertility sometimes so much so that we ignore the more important cues to beneficial qualities in a modern mate. Third, and most importantly, just when you discover useful cues they change. Our relevant environment is largely comprised of our fellow creatures, all of which are evolving new cues and new responses all the time. If we were to stop looking for new cues to what matters, the world would get ahead of us. So even if we could find the perfect cues they wouldn't last.

Attend vs. Ignore

How it comes up:

If cue X proves significant, then (if cue X, then do plan A, but if not cue X then do Plan B.)

Getting it wrong:

False positive: Attending to irrelevant cues.

False negative: Ignoring relevant cues.

Too sure: Not wondering whether to attend to a cue when wondering would be useful.

Too unsure: Wondering whether to attend to a cue when doubt isn't useful.

Whirrings at Night:

"She says she loves me still, but maybe she doesn't mean it. I mean, it's easy to mouth the words. Her eyes. When she looks away, that's her real answer, or is it?"

"They seemed so enthusiastic, but maybe I shouldn't take this job. My astrologer said it's an inauspicious time to sign contracts."

"First day at the new job and I'm sick to my stomach. Maybe it's a sign."

"Interest rates were down so I decided it was time to jump in. How was I to know the market would plummet?"

What they'll call you, if you:

	Guess no	**Guess yes**
Prove Right	Carefree Efficient Unflappable	Alert Sensitive Careful
Prove Wrong	Inattentive Oblivious Clueless	Over-sensitive Obsessive Over-reactive

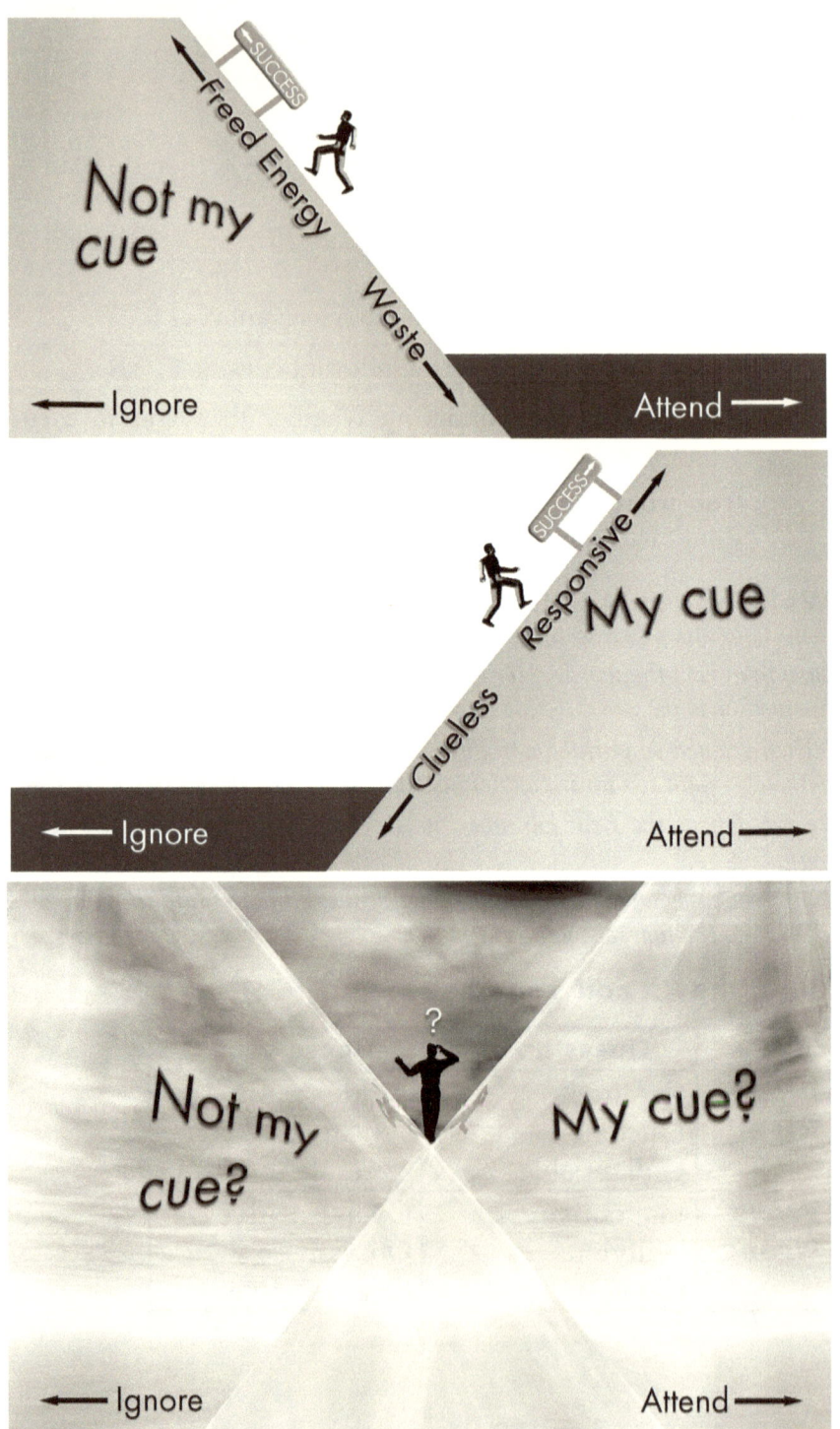

Just fork-edit:

'Always trust your intuition'

Sure there are lots of cues in this world, but there's only one you really need. Your intuition. Trust it. It knows what's best.

How does this work? There's something inside you called intuition, and it's got the teacher's answer key for all tests. All you've got to do is shut up and listen. It will whisper the answers to you. The answer key is right inside of you.

Where? It's in your gut. Sounds emotional. Is it your emotions? Do your emotions always have the right answer? Pain says, "don't," and pleasure says, "do." Is that how intuition works? It can't be. What about the times that pleasure says do but you shouldn't do, or pain said don't but you should. What about the pleasure of heroin, the pain of hard useful work?

Your intuition is more than your gut. It doesn't rely on rationality or your ego or your emotions. It's something you channel from a higher force.

Life's longing for the wisdom to know the difference—it's very strong. Strong enough that in movie-making creatures like us there is bound to be some well worn movie footage of depicting the dream of the longing getting fulfilled once and for all. Footage of ultimate satisfaction is simply what we get when we cross appetite with a mind that can picture things. You get "Mr. or Ms. Right"—a soon–to–arrive beloved, guru, God, parent, or genius residing inside your gut.

Now just because we have the appetite and aptitude to imagine a source of ultimate satisfaction, it doesn't necessarily mean that ultimate satisfaction is just a figment of our imagination, but it does call into question the assertion that because we can imagine it, it must exist.

And even the fact that many people imagine ultimate satisfaction the same way is not evidence that it must exist. A starving child can and will picture a banquet. A nation of starving people may be able to picture the same banquet, but the fact that they all can imagine it doesn't mean that the banquet is forthcoming. We all would like to know what to do and sometimes feel starved for clear certainty about what would be the right thing to do; hence the prevalence in the mind's eye of pictures of our hunger satiated.

What then is intuition really? Like consciousness, it's what we say it is. It could stand for this dreamed-for ability to tap into an all-knowing consciousness. Or, to represent something more likely to exist, we can say that intuition is just another name for the adaptive toolkit—your wisdom to know the difference, handy for addressing the omnipresent wonderings. It's not as exciting as having the master answer book embedded in your solar plexus, but it's still pretty exciting, this possession of a toolkit refined over three and a half billion years and further refined through your living experience—a toolkit that is among the very few lucky ones to have made it these three and a half billion years.

Your intuition is smart, otherwise you wouldn't be as far along as you are today. But no, it's not always right.

But the alternative definition of intuition as all knowing can be a very helpful tool in a Spin doctor's black bag: According to the Spin doctor's Hippocratic Oath, once we've made a decision, we should feel free to spin the heck out of it, as a way to galvanize ourselves and others to the decision we've made. When selectively applied as decision-affirmation, "always trust your gut" can be a great galvanizer. We make a decision and to stick with it, we say it has been endorsed by our deepest intuition, and it's always right. To make this employment of the omniscient gut plausible requires a simple trick of selectivity: Every time we make a decision that turns out well, credit it to our intuition. Every time a decision turns out poorly, say that we failed to consult our gut. We'll get 100% affirmation that intuition is the cue of choice. Though this is like shooting random arrows and then painting bull's-eyes around them wherever they've landed, it is a perfectly honorable way to make decisions, and many people—even very successful decision-makers—do just that.

Trusting our gut as an absolute source of wisdom gets us in trouble when our gut contradicts someone else's equally entrusted gut. Gut-trusting is perhaps the most common source of pigheadedness. The reason it's still relatively safe to trust our gut is that even if we were to subscribe to a philosophy that our gut knows all the right answers, our appetite for better answers will still, more often than not, outweigh our appetites for certainty. That is, whether you treat your gut as omniscient, or just your adaptive toolkit, you can't resist looking for what to do under different circumstances and which cues will tip you off as to which circumstances your are facing.

Take It Personally (T.I.P.)

The hungry are soon eaten.

We hunger for good cues. As mentioned earlier, our excitement about a good cue source (e.g., a charismatic guru) is first and foremost a testament to our appetite for cue sources and not to the actual practical benefits of that cue source can provide. An obsession with a specific cue can help you focus on what counts, but it can also be dangerous. One danger is vulnerability to predators.

Suppose you really want to find a spouse. Chances are you'll have a vision of what you're looking for pretty firmly in mind—the cue that will signal that you have found Mr. or Ms. Right. The more hungry you are to find him or her, the more firmly you'll hold the cue in mind which means you'll be hyper receptive should he or she come around, but it can also mean you'll be too receptive even if he or she doesn't. The hungrier we are, the more it shows on our faces. Hungry enough and our search criterion will flash brightly across our foreheads, "I'm looking for my soul mate. He [She] looks like this." Anyone who wants anything from you can read the cue off your forehead and act out what you are looking for. Hungry as you are to find someone who matches your search cue, you may overlook cues that you're dealing with an impostor.

This comes up in business all the time. A negotiator who can't walk away from the table is destined to make a poor deal. Who can't walk away from the table? The negotiators who are so hungry for what's on it that they've lost their peripheral vision. By obsessing over the cue, they become clueless.

Those who played hyper-hungry and lost as a result can rebound from one dangerous obsession to another. If one is badly burnt for having focused on one cue, a contrasting 180-degree opposite cue can become a subsequent obsession. The Military strategist Karl Von Clauswitz said that warriors tend to favor whatever strategy would have saved them in the previous battle. Rebounding after a painful divorce, spouses look for mates as different as possible from their previous spouses. Like double or nothing betting, they may actually do worse on the rebound because it's not the particular cues but the severity of the appetite that undid them. Rebounding full of a won't-get-fooled-again attitude, their reform campaign may become a painful case of I-once-was-lost-but-now-I'm blind.

The Sixth Wondering of the Ancient World:

How Do I Move This?

Aversion (push) and attraction (pull) make the world go round in our galaxy, our galaxy in the universe, electrons in atoms, atoms in molecules, friends in your circle, ideas in your head. You find some people fun, others a drag. Some ideas are appealing, others unpleasant. Life is a web of pushes and pulls.

Living things are like planets, suspended and orbiting under the influence of each other's gravitational tugs and shoves. Think of the constellation of motives that compel you to act as you do. Rarely is there a single motive unconstrained. For example, we are attracted toward our hobbies and recreations but don't spend our whole day at them because we are counter-attracted and compelled by a variety of duties and obligations.

Life can't help but employ the old push-and-pull to motivate behavior between beings. Mating, predation, parasitism, and mutualism all entail some combination of compelling pushes and enticing pulls. Males perform a mating dance to attract females who are either drawn in or push away the males. Parasites pull for influence over their host's bodies. The host resists, attempting to expel the parasite. Fungus and algae pull mutually on each other, forming the symbiotic organism called lichen. Living things are all creatures of their environment. Sure, our environment includes inanimate stuff like weather and rocks, but mostly it's made up of other creatures. Life plays cat and mouse, pursuit and flight, as one creature tries to transform another for its own purposes.

On the continuum between strong push and strong pull there are weaker pushes and pulls. The weak ones can be so weak as to be negligible, like the pull upon the earth of a star so far away that its influence can't be measured. Unlike the other wonderings this one therefore can be thought of as consisting of not two but three options: push, pull, and the neutral state in-between in which the push and pull are so negligible or mutually-canceling that they aren't perceived at all.

What are your choices when you face a persistently unpleasant pull? You can try to get out of its way, you can fight it, or you can work with it, trying to change the system from within. In politics these options go by the names *voice, exit,* and *loyalty*. In predator-prey relations they are called *fight, flight,* and *subordination*.

Oddly enough, sex originates not in attraction but in aversion. Sex's main advantage over cloning as a way of producing offspring is that it makes it harder for this year's parasites to damage next year's offspring. With sex, the offspring are half like Mom and half like Dad, not exactly the same as either of them alone. Having kids different from yourself keeps the parasite that worked on you from working as successfully on your offspring, which means your child has a better chance of getting through Mother Nature's sifter. Competing successfully with a parasite, the parents cooperate in sexuality.

People generally associate evolutionary biology with a pushy battle for survival. There's truth to this depiction, but only a half-truth. Creatures are often more effective at pushing when they pull together. So we see phenomenally intricate and clever collaborations throughout natural systems.

Some people, offended by the way evolutionary theory has depicted life as unappetizingly competitive, argue that nature is much more lovingly cooperative than it is competitive. It's very difficult to quantify the amount of competition and cooperation in life in part because most competition occurs between forces that are themselves cohesively cooperative entities. After all, if you haven't got it together, it's no contest.

The fact is, cooperation and competition both exist. The often-heated debate about whether life is more cooperative or competitive gets its warmth from our heated search for cues for how we should act. But the ratio of competition to cooperation in nature is not a great cue. Morality is local to each species. Humans have more ways and reasons to be cooperative than the majority of other living creatures. We are social animals with a unique capacity for mental movie making, which as mentioned earlier enables us to hold ourselves to acquired commitments more readily than any other creature. It also enables us to imagine alternatives to our commitments, which is why we lose more sleep to doubt than other creatures. Still, we use our unique capacity to reinforce our commitments largely to commit ourselves to other people. So who cares how competitive nature is. We've got our own issues and options.

Push vs. Pull

The sixth wondering is the behavioral complement to all the wonders that came before. For example, the first wondering of the ancient world is whether to join something or not, and depending on one's answer and the answer of whatever one is considering joining, a dance of push and pull ensues. Dancing toward something that's dancing away from you, what are you going to do? Try to push it into a corner where it has to dance with you? Try to pull it toward you? Try to act as though you don't care, hoping that it comes to you? These strategies are age-old as is the question life has had to answer again and again about which of these is most likely to pay off.

Push vs. Pull

How it comes up:

If cue X, then push.

If cue Y, then pull.

Getting it wrong:

False positive: Pushing when you should pull.

False negative: Pulling when you should push.

Too sure: Not wondering which to do when it would be helpful to think about.

Too unsure: Wondering which to do when it's not going to improve your strategy to pay it any more attention.

Whirrings at night:

Am I being too tough? Is it only going make them fight back?
Am I being too kind? Will they think I'm needy?
Why can't I control my temper?
Why am I such an easy mark?
Is there any way I can get him to come along on this deal?
What if we draw the line and they cross it?
What if we don't draw the line and they walk all over us?

What they'll call you, if you:

	Push	Pull
Prove **Right**	Powerful	Diplomatic
	Formidable	Generous
	Firm	Kind
Prove **Wrong**	Aggressive	Manipulative
	Angry	A Push-over
	Dictatorial	Naïve

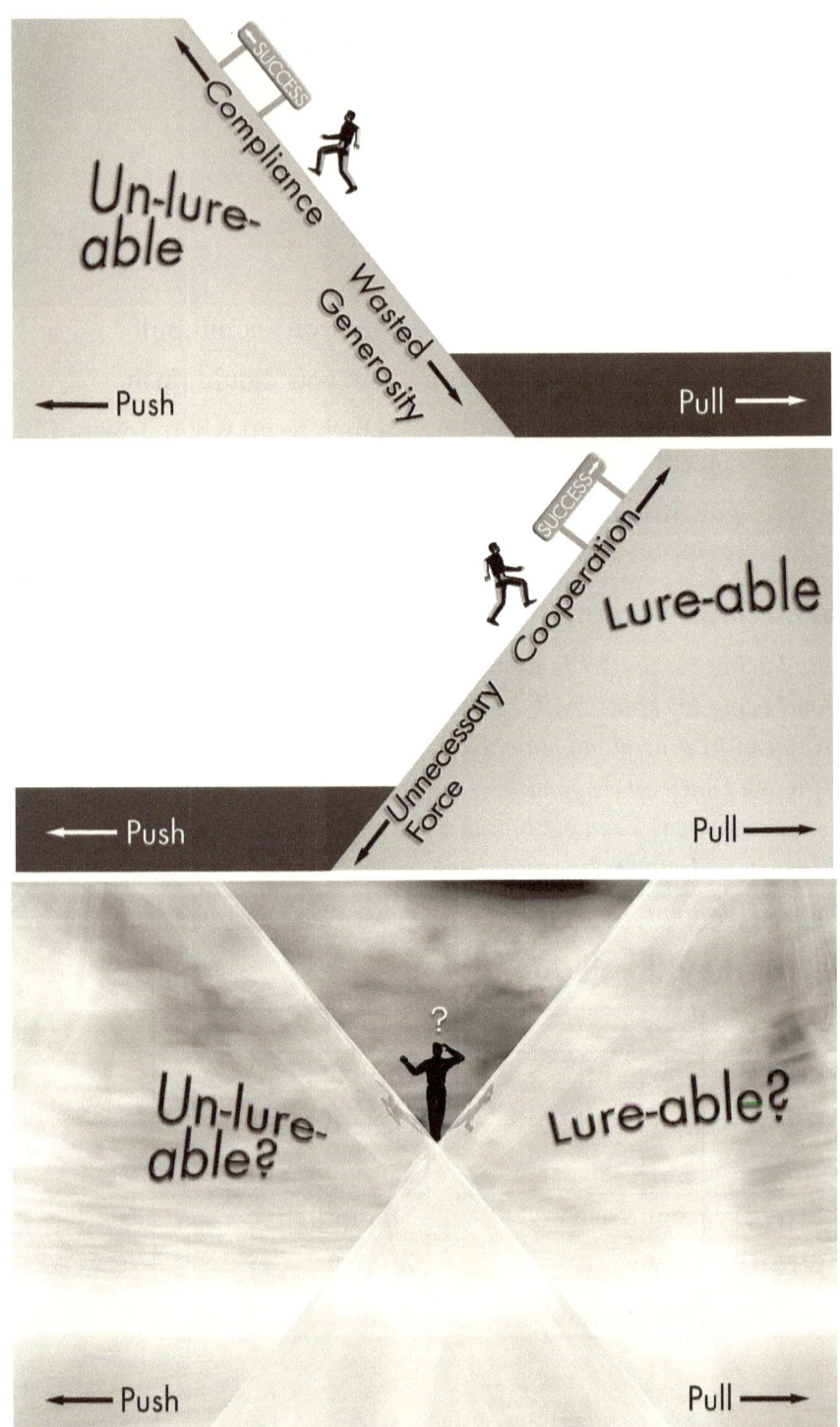

Just fork-edit:

'Love is always the solution'

"You catch more flies with honey than vinegar'

'An eye for an eye leaves the world blind'

'Turn the other cheek'

Statements like these argue for pull over push, cooperation over resistance or defection. They are useful for counterbalancing a tendency to move toward pushing first. Anger, bullying, blaming, and shaming—reactions well within the human repertoire—all inflict pain as a way of influencing each other's behavior. When two bodies get started inflicting pain in mutual retaliation, a spiraling arm's race results. Since these are messy we need ways to keep them in check. In many animal species, males compete for their females, but few compete to the death. Though they'll kill members of other species and clearly have the capacity to fight to the death, something compels them to toggle off their to-the-death belligerence when fighting each other. It's not species preservation but it is in the interest of each individual to avoid escalating battles. We humans accumulate moral mechanisms to limit our own capacity for such escalation, and these choose-love absolutes can come in handy.

People generally have an ambivalent (you could say push/pull) relationship with the idea of retaliation, harboring conflicting beliefs that it is both a fair response but also a problematic one. Studies in the field of game theory suggest that a strategy like tit-for-tat—responding to a push with an equal and opposite push—is a practical way to balance generosity and protectiveness.

If every time someone "tatted" you, you "titted" back in equal measure and the person who "tatted" you recognized that it was all you were doing, and so didn't tit back, then we wouldn't have arms races. There are two primary reasons that it is messier than that.

First, it is hard to retaliate in equal measure. Often retaliators retaliate a little extra for good measure. Second, it is hard for both sides to measure the force of each push by a consistent standard so there is a big problem with the misinterpretation of tats. What if you think you have been pushed when you haven't? If you retaliate, it looks like a first strike that justifies a retaliation. The result is that each side is convinced that the other side started with first strikes that both sides deny making. Many conflicts in playrooms, bedrooms, boardrooms, or war rooms escalate this way.

We need cultural mechanisms that enable us to counteract the hair-trigger sense that the other side provoked us. So it is no wonder that we would want to have sayings that help us err on the side of niceness. Counting to ten before striking back, not sending poison pen letters until you have had a chance to sleep on it, turning the other cheek—we need these ways to temper hot tempers.

But just because we have a tendency to misconstrue an innocuous gesture as a slight doesn't mean there are no slights in this world.

While it's true that with real flies, real honey, and real vinegar, honey works best, but who wants to catch flies? Maybe the saying is apt but reversed as a case for using vinegar. Flies are parasites. To what extent does a policy of universal invitational pull and cooperation help? Doesn't honey keep the parasites coming back for more?

Yes, an eye for an eye may leave the world blind. But does the statement make a complete case against all retribution? It can't. Imagine trying to apply it if someone really took your own child's eye out. A saying like this is most convincing when you don't really think about what it means when someone takes an eye.

And so we are left to wonder, what is the best response when we feel we've been slighted. Sometimes at night, you may lie in bed fuming, wondering whether to resist like a snarling dog, whether to absorb it, or whether to get out of harm's way.

Take It Personally (T.I.P.)

I never do anything for just one reason; it never has just one effect. Life is like playing piano with oven mitts on.

Picture yourself as a planet suspended in orbit by the tugs and pressures of many other planetary bodies. Think of these other bodies as the people and ideas that have an influence on you, pushing you toward certain actions and away from others; pulling you this way and that.

Whenever you consider making a move, you can feel the pushes and pulls of their force fields upon you. Even when you are staying on course, following your natural trajectory through your options, these other bodies are setting your course. And when one of them shifts course it alters that balance among forces. A force field gets stronger and influences you more or gets weaker and influences you less. Think of how when one planet moves, all the other planets in its gravitational field register a shift in the tugs that hold them in place, adjusting everything's balance with everything else.

Anything you do, any shift in position, generally causes a variety of other effects—some intended; others unintended

Think about how this planetary you is a conglomeration too of parts held together by internal pushes and pulls. Henry Thoreau wrote, "I am a parcel of vain strivings tied by a chance bond together . . . Their links were made so loose and wide, methinks, for milder weather." Like the molecular structure of a planet, you are comprised internally of many pushes and pulls, cohesively and antagonistically interacting with yourself.

Now notice that more often than not, we talk about a single push or pull rather than the whole messy constellation. In explaining our choices we say, "The reason is..." more often than we say "the reasons are." But the reason rarely "is." There are more pushes and pulls than we can possibly keep track of. Under the influence of so many pushes and pulls, life becomes like playing piano with oven mitts on. You go to hit one note and a bunch of neighboring notes play too.

Then why, if there are multiple tugs, do we say, "The reason is," more often than we say, "The reasons are?"

For simplicity's sake—we can't afford to keep track of all the details. We are constantly compacting and boxing up explanations, packaging up lots of detailed recorded mental movie footage and storing them in memory's boxes with simple labels. But it's not just simplicity we seek. How we remember what motivated us to choose one action or another has a big effect on how we behave in the future. When we claim to have done something for just one reason and with just one effect, there is very often a pragmatic strategic reason for labeling our motives the way we do.

And speaking of motivated simplicity, think for a moment about the ultimate box label. The one they'll affix to your coffin. If you ever lie awake at night wondering if you'll be able to look back at the end of your life and say, "Yes, I've lived well," take comfort from the fact that with motivation to maintain a positive story about your past, you'll probably be able to interpret and label your life favorably regardless of how you've lived—even more so if your memory gets worse with age.

You may have heard the assertion that you create your own reality by your thoughts. If our thoughts had the power to change things all over the globe thereby changing our reality, think of what a crowded galaxy of pushes and pulls we'd orbit in. The mechanisms whereby an individual could do this would add considerable complexity to the world of cause and effect. The people who argue that we have that kind of influence on our reality often state this general case before pinpointing a specific result of such causality: "We create our own reality, so I know my thoughts about my business partner made him do the wrong thing."

Of course, it is possible that there are unseen forces shaping our reality, even ones emanating from us. But there's something funny about positing magnitudes more causal interconnected complexity and in the same breath claiming to be more capable of pinpointing specific strands of causality. It's like saying, "The two main highways are blocked and traffic is 100 times more snarled than usual, so I know that I'll get to work today at exactly 8:36."

Given how little conscious attention we can afford to expend on explaining any one of our behaviors, when we wonder what causes us to act, we generally look for a single reason and when we find it, we move on. Mostly this is a very efficient way to operate. It only sometimes gets us into trouble; for example, when you confront a colleague about an error he made and suggest a possible explanation for it that your colleague would rather not consider, your colleague can counter that he already knows the single reason why he did what he did. Explanation found; case closed. You may try to force the door open, but a single explanation is an effective dead bolt. Reminding ourselves that we never do anything for just one reason can help to keep our minds ajar, if not altogether open, to our multiple motives.

The Seventh Wondering of the Ancient World:

Is There A Win/Win Solution?

Though at the very start of this book we acknowledged that life is certainly not all doubt, ambiguity, ambivalence, and the hand-wringing strain of making tough judgment calls, it may have occurred to you throughout the litany of doubts that followed that it may all be much ado about nothing. Why does it have to be either-or? Maybe it's both/and. Sometimes we think were stuck between two horns of a dilemma but the third horn is really what we're looking for. What about false dichotomies? Maybe we doubt and worry too much. The seventh wondering of the ancient world is whether there really is a dilemma or not. A real dilemma is a win-lose situation in which there are real trade-offs—more of one thing means less of another. A false dilemma is a win-win situation disguised as a win-lose. It doesn't look like there's a way to have your cake and eat it too, but there really is.

Some problems are like jigsaw puzzles. There is a solution that puts everything in its place. Others aren't. No matter how you configure things, there's always potential for improvement. With each of the wonderings so far, on the list of ways of betting wrong there have been two ways listed that are wonderings of the seventh kind. Called Too Sure and Too Unsure. These are errors one level up from the dilemma in question: Am I assuming this a dilemma when it isn't one? Am I assuming this isn't a dilemma when it really is? We all know what it's like to overlook something that proved significant, and to worry over something that took care of itself. If only we could always tell the true from the false dichotomies.

It may be hard to imagine that the strictly biological systems of the ancient world dealt with this wonder. Mother Nature doesn't ever "feel" stuck, wishing for solutions and wondering whether they are possible. She wonders by experiment, trying things out in the real world. She hasn't got any foresight and does no what-if theorizing, and she's got all the time in the world. She has come up with vastly more brilliant solutions to problems than we humans have, but she did it by trial and error, mindless sifting over millions of configurations of things at once, and over more time than we can possible imagine. So how could she wonder whether a situation is win-win or win-lose?

As touched upon in previous wonders, living things have to accumulate the wherewithal to figure out who is a competitor and who is a collaborator, which is a kind of judgment call about win-win games and win-lose. Another kind of wonder is implied in the relationship between what biologists call form and function. Here's an example:

Wheels are very useful—so useful, you'd think that evolution would have invented them long ago. Why aren't there creatures getting around on wheels instead of legs?

There are a few but they're microscopic. They don't have wheels but they do have axles of sorts—little whipping tails that rotate freely in sockets. And then you've got things like your shoulder's rotator cuff, which enables you to spin your arms almost like a windmill.—almost but not completely in smooth rotation like a wheel. Why no true wheels? Why not some creature that takes rotator cuffs a step further, exchanging arm bones for round disks that roll like the wheels of all-terrain vehicles? Dinosaur wheels— they could have been so functional.

Well, there's a technical problem. To spin freely the wheel can't be fully connected to the axle, but body parts require circulation so they have to be connected. This is an example of a physical constraint—form—limiting what functions can evolve.

In biology, there's a fundamental tension between function and form, between could-be-useful and would-be-possible. Physical, genetic, and historical constraints limit what adaptations can arise. Mother Nature does what she can with what she's dealt. The form question is, "What's dealt?" The function question is, "What can it be used for?"

In wondering how to make the most of what you're dealt, you deal daily with questions of form and function and the relationship between them. Sometimes looking at the form things have taken in your life, you may not been able to see a damned thing more you can do with them. As the saying goes, you can't get blood from a turnip.

If you had asked Mother Nature 100 million years ago, "What about wheels?" she would have replied like the discouraging old geezer at the rural gas station, "You can't get there from here." It's win-lose. You want wheels? Then you can't have circulation. You want circulation? Then you can't have wheels.

But can't you? There's more than one way to skin the proverbial cat. We humans now have wheels and they sprouted out where you'd least expect them—not from our limbs but from our heads. Mother Nature couldn't turn legs into wheels, but in a very roundabout way she eventually got to them through the evolutionary modification of our brains which enabled us to make wheels along with a lot of other extensions to the toolkit that biological evolution endowed us with. It goes to show, you never can tell.

Did our fancy brains evolve so that we could make wheels? There's plenty of speculation as to why we got our fancy brains and why, if they're so fancy, other creatures don't have them. The speculations have a lot to do with form and function—what is possible and what would be useful. But of course they did not evolve simply so we could have wheels. We use our brains for so many things.

Though Mother Nature has come up with some very ingenious uses for what she's dealt, she has done so by a very nearsighted process. She is not good at planning ahead. Her manifest ingenuity isn't the product of forethought, but of the vast stretches of time over which she has sifted by trial and error through a variety of tools, accumulating the keepers.

In fact, Mother Nature is both nearsighted and strict. If a trait isn't immediately useful, it doesn't filter through her sifter. Every trick in the book—every adaptive trait that every living creature possesses—had to remain useful throughout its entire duration in the creature's toolkit. Even something as intricate as an eye—back when all it was good for was crude light sensitivity—if that light sensitivity wasn't useful to a creature's survival and reproduction, it wouldn't have been a keeper—it wouldn't have lasted long enough to get as intricate as it has become. One false move—one generation without offspring—and the whole future family line gets it. Today's underachiever with great future potential will not survive Mother Nature's sifting to ever realize its potential.

This strictness might seem discouraging. It suggests that Mother Nature needed a whole lot of time to accumulate as many good tools as she has. She has had a lot of time, but she has a few other things going for her as well.

First, as strict as she is about maintaining utility at all times, she is very lenient about what kind of utility it is. Mother Nature isn't particular about what hole in her sieve a tool pops through, so long as it pops through one hole or another.

A tool that proved useful by one standard before may prove useful by another standard later. Your ear's stirrup bone started out as the bone that supported a fish's gill. A lizard doesn't need a gill support; by the time lizards evolved, this same bone proved useful as one piece of a two-piece jawbone. Your jawbone is a one-piece affair which frees that old gill arch to become the ear's stirrup. The tool passed from function to function, like a monkey letting go of one branch in time to grab another. In this sense, necessity isn't just the mother of brand new inventions. Necessity is also the child inheriting and appropriating old inventions.

Like a crowd gathering around an interesting invention, functions can gather around on existing forms. Your mouth was originally useful for eating, but now you use it for breathing, talking, and kissing. Bird feathers were first useful as insulation and then became useful for flight also.

This same flexible utilization works in human invention too. Think of how many new uses we've discovered for computers. Think of all the things you started to do for one reason and later found you were doing for other reasons. For example, many guys took up hobbies to impress the girls but now pursue them for other reasons. The hobbies have taken on lives of their own. Some say that the original engine of cognitive development was for mating—brainchildren as a way of increasing your odds of producing real children. But our fascination with brainchildren has taken on a life of its own.

One of Mother Nature's most effective ways to innovate is by making multiple copies of existing forms within a single creature and then finding new specialized uses for the copies. Lobsters have multiple copies of the same form—a segment with two opposing limbs. Each copy has become a specialist at some function—legs, egg-movers, food shovelers, claws—there's more than one way to use a pair of opposing limbs. In this respect, the variety of things that feed Mother Nature's sieve don't just vary in quality, they vary in quantity. If a tool proves useful, Mother Nature is likely to make multiple copies of it and find out what else it can be used for. So while Mother Nature has no foresight, she does make educated guesses—applying something that worked in one situation to another, on the "hunch" that it might work there too.

Form constrains function while function shapes form. Your ear bone's form constrains the functions that can be made of it, and yet it is no longer shaped like the original gill arch but has adapted to its new function in hearing. The relationship between form and function is dialectical, which in this context means a relationship in which two things shape each other. A shapes B while B shapes A.

Being dialectically intertwined, form and function are hard to untangle. In trying to imagine whether you can achieve some new function, you'll look to existing form for cues. Form is what you are dealt—what the past has brought into the present. That form is as good a cue to the future as you are going to get, but it is far from perfect. So we are often left to wonder.

Fight vs. Cooperate

How it comes up:

If cue A then fight.

If cue B then cooperate.

Getting it wrong:

False positive: Cooperating with a fighter.

False negative: Fighting with a cooperater.

Too sure: Assuming it's one or another when you'd do well to wonder.

Too unsure: Doubting whether you've read it right when you have.

Whirrings at Night:

Am I settling for a compromise when there's really a better way?
Am I holding out for an agreement when in fact there isn't one possible?
I thought we were in this together. What happened?
How could I overlook such a perfect solution to our problems?
Why do I always assume the other guy is out to get me?
Why did I let them take advantage of me?

What they'll call you, if you:

	Cooperate	Fight
Prove Right	Cooperative Creative Altruistic	Practical Prudent Realistic
Prove Wrong	Naïve Idealistic Gullible	Cold Paranoid Agressive

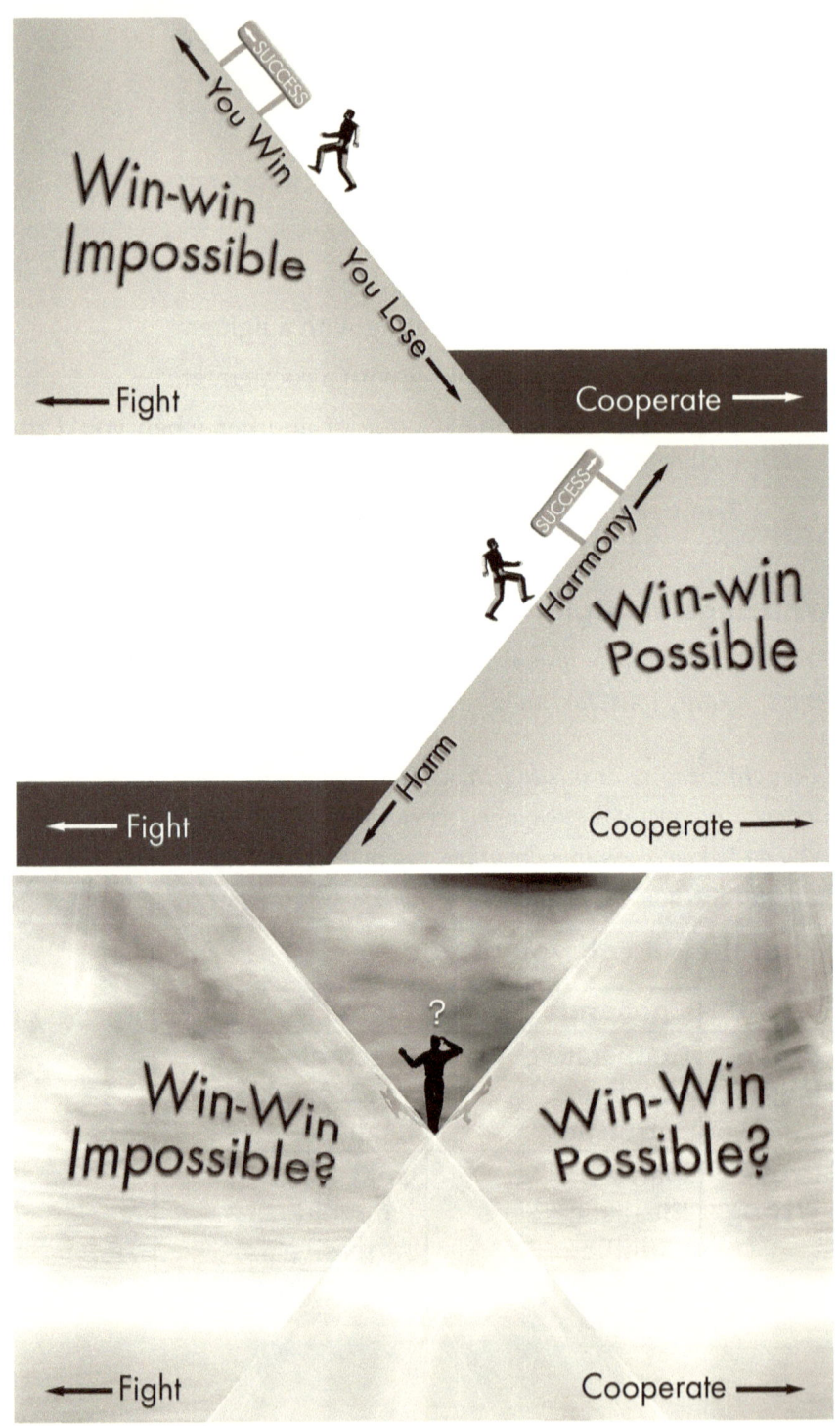

Just fork-edit:

'It's hard wired'
'The only constant is change'

In some circles a book like this would be considered dangerous because it taps biology for insights into human nature. In other circles people are increasingly comfortable calling all sorts of human traits "biologically hard wired."

The nature/nurture debate lives on, in spite of many scientists' attempts to put it to rest with arguments that it's both in dialectical interaction with nature shaping nurture and nurture shaping nature.

Everyone who weighs in on the nature/nurture debate tends to argue from some kind of scientific authority as though the debate were about facts. It's mostly not. It is rarely a purely scientific question that's being debated but rather an engineering one—social engineering. What makes the nature/nurture debate a debate is the way it bears on the seventh wondering—form and function. What form does human nature take and how does that limit what we could become?

Most of us hope that humans can become much more than we are. In the last three hundred years, we've gained dangerous power over our environment. Along with that power we've gain the capacity to see and measure the danger. Most of us hope that one way or another we'll be able to change human behavior and avert the danger.

Science got us into this mess. Maybe science can help us get out of it. Maybe biological science—the science that describes our natural forms and established functions—can inform beneficent social engineering so that our great-great grandchildren can live less dangerous than we do today. Maybe studying form will give us a clear picture of what won't change so we don't waste energy trying to change what we can't. Maybe it will give us handles on what people really want so we can employ existing forms for better functions.

If we want to negotiate with ourselves and win, we need to understand our nature—which means discovering which of our motives are, and are not negotiable.

So what does biology reveal?

Well there are those who say it reveals a lot, and that what it shows is discouraging. It turns out that the seven deadly sins are in our genes. We're hard wired for nastiness and we might as well face it.

Reacting to this interpretation others say we should not look to biology at all. We aren't hard wired for anything, it's nurture that determines who we are and, thank god, because while nothing biological is negotiable, everything in nurture is. Simply change the culture and you'll change human nature.

There are still others who say that biology reveals a lot and that what it shows is encouraging. The natural world is full of harmony and synergy, organisms cooperating with each other and ecologies in balance. The seven Godly virtues are in our genes. We were born to live in harmony, but culture, some appalling frozen accident, has corrupted us. Relatively speaking that's a minor problem, because nurture can be changed. Nature cannot.

Each of these positions is useful and to some degree credible. It's especially useful though to step back from the debate and notice that *nature* has become a code word for what can't change. *Nurture* becomes a code word for what can.

If nature then can't change.

If nurture then can change.

But no amount of both/and efforts to quell the debate will quell it until we recognize that what really drives it is the need to know what we can and can't change—which of human nature's newly necessary functions we'll be able to squeeze out of what we're dealt.

Much as we'd like nature to nurture to serve as reliable cues, they aren't. As we've already seen there's plenty of flexibility in nature. And there are things about the nurture that we've had during the course of our lifetimes that cannot and will not change over what remains of it.

All the arguments that what is should be—that we can't use such and such a tool in such and such a way because that's not how it was meant to be used, that if God had wanted us to drive he would have give us wheels, and that biology hard-wires us for certain behaviors—should be taken with a heaping teaspoon of salt. It ain't necessarily so.

And on the other hand, the currently popular saying that the only constant is change can't be true either. Another constant is constancy. That is, some things never change. The form things take may or may not change; so another thing that's constant is wondering about what we can do with what we're dealt and whether there is a better way around the corner we just haven't noticed yet.

Take It Personally (T.I.P.)

Which came first, the thinking or the ache?

In dialectical processes, A causes B and B causes A. Form and function are entangled, one of the reasons why their relationship can be confusing. Dialectical relationships make it hard to pinpoint the prime mover. Which came first, the chicken or the egg? Since eggs hatch chickens and chickens lay eggs, it's hard to know.

There may be no more visceral experience of dialectical processes than the relationship between emotion and thought. A dark thought can induce the physical discomfort of an emotional ache, but likewise, a physical sensation of heartache can induce a dark thought. Unsettled thoughts can give you a stomachache, but a stomachache caused by indigestion can also make us think unsettled thoughts. Sometimes it's hard to know which came first: the thinking or the ache.

With two points of entry into the vicious cycle, there are two primary ways to intervene and interrupt it. One is by interrupting the ache, the other by interrupting the thoughts.

Sometimes, describing the ache as a physical sensation is enough to interrupt the cycle. What feels like full-blown terror, when noticed with some objectivity, can merely appear as a vibrant tingling in the chest—an alarm that on closer inspection isn't blaring but buzzing. Something about describing it plainly neutralizes some of its assumed implications and therefore its power to compel dark thoughts.

Interrupting dark thoughts means replacing them with lighter ones, like picking yourself up by the scruff of your neck and moving yourself to other vistas. This is the basis of cognitive therapy. If you can change your thoughts, the physical sensation sometimes follows suit.

A third approach is to simply let the dialectical relationship play itself out: Assume that there's nothing to change, no need to intervene. Treat an emotional downturn like bad weather that comes and goes and needs no explanation and requires no remedy.

The Seven Wonderings of the Modern World

Enough biology. We're humans after all. We've got our own dilemmas custom-built for creatures with our particular kinks.

We're movie makers and by that token we're also commuters shuttling between two worlds at once—the vast and expanding mind's eye movie palace in which we can imagine anything and the real one outside that doesn't always live up to our movie-land dreams.

No other organism on earth experiences our bi-planetary existence, so we're on our own, pioneering whole new ways of life. We are self-reflective creatures, able to dream the impossible dream that would be really impossible for other creatures.

Our new ways have certainly helped us deal with wonderings of the ancient world. We bring our cogni-cinematic brilliance to bear on problems that would stump a potato bug. But we pay a price.

So now, the seven wonderings of the modern (human) world. You'll no doubt recognize them all.

The First Wondering of the Modern World:

How Long Should I Wait?

The mind's eye is an adaptive tool that proved useful from the get-go. It has accumulated a phenomenal quantity of uses, and it's a keeper, in part because it allows you to picture and then work toward goals in a way that no other creature can.

Imagining future successes, you can delay gratification, enduring less now for more later. You can endure five years of medical school torture by picturing in your mind's eye what it will be like to finally become a successful doctor. You can court that attractive person for months, suffering all sorts of rejection, by picturing the two of you eventually becoming a happily married couple. Delayed gratification is possible because you can keep your mind's eye on the prize even when your real eye can't see it.

This kind of delayed gratification, which entails more than just waiting but actually throwing yourself headlong into disadvantage as a way to get at some future advantage, opens up opportunities to humans that other species miss.

A chimp offered a choice between two pieces of fruit invariably chooses the larger one. If you reverse the experiment, giving him the piece of fruit he doesn't choose, he can't learn to pick the smaller piece. He still picks the larger piece, even if as a result he gets the smaller one. He can't make the subtle paradoxical move of choosing the small piece in order to get the bigger one because he can't work backward from the future state to the present choice as easily as we humans can.

A dog on a tangled leash yanks outward and barks. He wants a longer leash so he pulls, unable to make the paradoxical move in toward the tangle in order to release the entanglement. If you found yourself tangled, you might yank once or twice, but noticing that the leash was coming up short, you'd stop take one look around, make a quick mental movie of the sequence to full disentanglement and make the paradoxical move inward toward the tangle in order to regain enough leash to move outward.

The mind's eye is like X-ray vision that permits you to see through an obstacle to treasure on the other side, which motivates you to surmount the obstacle. If life were an Easter egg hunt and you were competing with nonhuman life forms to find the

132

candy eggs, your mind's eye would enable you to see eggs that the other living things wouldn't even know existed. This is one of the fundamental differences between human and nonhuman life. It's even a difference between how humans and Mother Nature make choices, since Mother Nature as explained above cannot plan ahead.

Still, it's not as though we've left the here and now behind. Present pain for later gain still hurts. We're only motivated to endure the pain sometimes and it's only worth it sometimes. That dogged non-paradoxical yanking on the leash persists in us. Dog is our copilot, and sometimes the dog is right. We shouldn't always hold out for long-term gain.

We humans are seeing-*I* dogs, who at least sometimes can step back to picture the big picture, make a mental movie of the self's long-term intent and make the paradoxical move or not, depending. We have an expanded repertoire that includes the direct and the paradoxical route to greater satisfaction. Wondering whether we should or shouldn't endure make paradoxical moves is therefore a uniquely human obsession and the first wonder of the modern world.

Should you go to medical school? Should you wait on her doorstep until she loves you? Which is better, the moment on the lips or having it not land forever on your hips? Should you quit smoking?

Since our path into the future is always cobbled with uncertainties, delaying gratification sounds easier than it really is. What we're really talking about is delayed uncertain gratification. A bird in the hand is worth two in the bush … on average anyway. The bird in the hand is worth only about half of the two in the bush if you're certain to catch both, but if you're not going to catch them, then that bird in the hand is worth infinitely more.

A fish can't keep itself from taking the dangling instant gratification of a worm on a hook even if it means death. You look at that bait and you hem and haw. Should I bite or shouldn't I? The real lure that dangles in front of your real eye competes with that shimmering ephemeral vision of a possible future lure that dangles before your mind's eye.

And so we wonder if that future lure is really worth all the work, or alternatively wonder why you don't have more self-discipline in resisting the immediate gratification.

Short-term vs. Long-term

How it comes up:

If cue X, then focus on short-term.

If cue Y, then focus on long-term.

Getting it wrong:

False positive: Holding out for long-term benefits when they aren't forthcoming.

False negative: Not holding out for long-term benefits when they are coming.

Too sure: Not questioning a decision to hold out when it's time to.

Too unsure: Wondering whether it's right to hold out when you are better off doing what you're doing.

Whirring at night:

I hope this is worth the sacrifice.
Why am I so impulsive?
What's wrong with eating the low-hanging fruit?
This is getting ridiculous. I don't think they're ever going to come through.
Sure, good things come to those who wait, but always?

What they'll call you, if you:

	Wait Short	**Wait long**
Prove **Right**	Practical	Patient
	Expeditious	Self-disciplined
	Efficient	Prudent
Prove **Wrong**	Impulsive	Doesn't know when to quit
	Irresponsible	Inflexible
	Impatient	

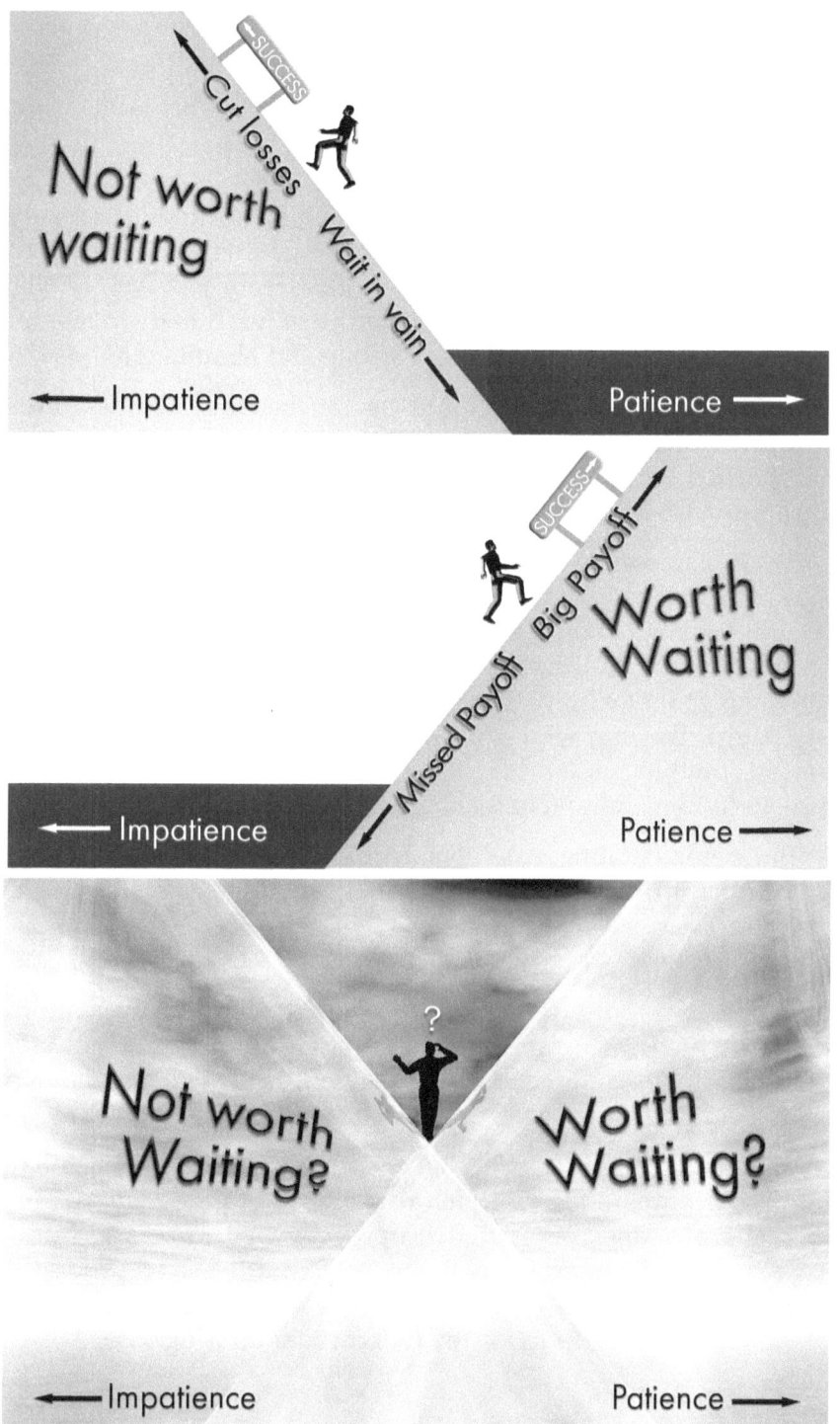

Just fork-edit:

'Don't be attached to outcomes'

'Live your goals'

What do you get when you cross preference with this uniquely human capacity for mental movie making? You get a movie of desire fulfilled. Your dream date. Your dream job. Mr. or Ms. Right. The perfect home. A goal, a picture of fulfillment. In mental movie makers like us, goals grow strong and abundant as weeds.

Some argue that they should be plucked like weeds. "Free yourself from illusions of ultimate fulfillment," they say. Don't be attached to outcomes. "Life is suffering," said the Buddha, attributing the suffering to these weeds.

What he meant is open to interpretation. A popular reading is that attachments, expectations, and goals are just bad stuff that accumulates but shouldn't. The people who make this argument on behalf of the Buddha continue to harbor goals, not least among them the goal of eliminating goals. The Buddha himself becomes Mr. Right, the one who got beyond coveting Ms. Right or the perfect anything. Keep him firmly in mind and you can match him, becoming enlightened and goal-free too.

But before pulling your weeds (as if you even could) check them for nutritional content. What, if anything, are they good for?

In the push and pull of life, a goal is a wonderful pull. It's orienting. The more compelling the pull, the harder you work to reach it, which is why many people emphatically assert the counter argument to the Buddha's, saying that you won't get anywhere in this world unless you embrace your goals completely.

Having Mr. Right in mind helps you find him or someone like him. You compare the man before your eyes to the man in your mental movie and if they match up pretty well, you say, "I do." This method produces many a good match. It has also produced many a bitterly unsatisfied single person who holds out for Mr. or Ms. Right, never settling for reality's meager offerings.

So are goals good or bad? Should you relax them or hold them firm? It depends. First, it depends on the goal. We're glad Martin Luther King Jr. was so goal-oriented. We regret that Adolph Hitler was.

Second, it depends on the goal's practical power to orient and disorient. A goal serves as a template, a tool to help you find things that fit in your life. Low tolerance for misfit can help you find good fits or make you such a perfectionist that you pass up the best that life in its imperfections has to offer.

Most of us have goals that are fairly well calibrated to what's available. When your goals get unrealistic, you find too few things that fit, and you naturally adjust by relaxing your goals. Yet all of us know at least one person who seems absolutely clueless about how far he or she is from reaching the goal. We might take some comfort from thinking that we are at least better calibrated than this person, but this person nonetheless provides disconcerting evidence as to just how clueless a person can get. How are we to know we aren't just like him or her? The question may not come up often, but on a bad day, you might feel like an impostor, a legend only in your own mind. Big hat, no cattle as the cowboys say; battleship mouth, rowboat ass, as the sailors say.

So at the margins of indecision, you wonder: "The reason I haven't gotten what I wanted—is my standard too high, or am I just too impatient?" And, much as it would help, there's no simple rule like "Always hold your goals lightly (or tightly)."

Take It Personally (T.I.P.)

Unless and until you have reached your goal, there's no certainty about whether it's reachable.

Pick any yes/no goal-oriented question that keeps you up at night that starts with "Can I" or "Will I."

Notice this about it: Unless and until its goal is reached, there is built-in ambiguity—you can't tell if you can reach it but haven't yet, or if you just plain can't. This ambiguity is extremely unnerving.

It becomes slightly less unnerving when you realize that the ambiguity comes with the territory of any goal-oriented behavior. Awareness of this might also keep the "Why me?" question at bay: Why you—why anybody? It's also an insurance policy against feeling like an idiot for trying to reach a goal you don't end up reaching. How could you know in advance that you couldn't reach it? While there are certainly riskier and safer bets, goal-oriented behavior is always betting.

The Second Wondering of the Modern World:

Is Something Amiss?

Having a mind's eye doesn't mean abandoning trial and error, but applying it in a much faster, more flexible medium. With natural selection, each creature is a trial and each error is a death. The dumb ideas become flesh, and the bodies get the heave-ho with the ideas—a tragic waste.

With mind's eye evolution your bad ideas get the heave-ho before you try them out in the real world, and your life is spared, which should please you no end. Trial and error takes place in your head; you selectively retain the winning ideas in the trial-and-error championships. The winning plans include both your goals and your plans for how to achieve them.

The mind's eye selectively retains your intentions. The form they take has three elements: an ultimate goal, a plan for reaching it, and expectations about what you'll find along the way, given your assumptions about what the path will be like.

Our expectations are like the canary that coal miners took down into mines as an early warning system. If the canary dies, the miner knows that poison gas is leaking in and get out quick. Similarly when your expectations—your mental movie of where you should be at certain stages in a long-term project—do not fit your outer reality, it alerts you that something might be amiss. Might be, after all, with dog as your copilot, you don't like the pain of delayed uncertain gratification much anyway. You're bound to feel that something's amiss sometimes even when it isn't.

Is there's poison gas in the coal mine or is your canary overreacting? When you aren't meeting expectations does it mean that your plans and goals need to be changed or that your expectations do? Is there something amiss? Maybe nothing is except your expectations. Or maybe something really is. Sometimes it's hard to tell and you wonder. This is the second wondering of the modern world, unique to humans because we alone among all species have the capacity to devise and maintain elaborate plans, goals, and expectations.

Change Plans vs. Change Expectations

You thought you would pass the bar exam on your first try and you didn't. You had given yourself four years to become a lawyer and you are now into your fifth. Were your expectations overly optimistic or is this a sign that you really weren't cut out to be a lawyer? Your marriage was supposed to be happier when the kids left home, but it is only more frustrating. Maybe it's a sign that you should revise your plan to live together forever, or maybe you just expect too much as usual and should be more tolerant of the world as it is.

Humans, with our capacity to imagine better states, experience a gap between where we are and where we'd like to be. People who study decision making call it the *aspirational gap*.

A big gap makes most of us uncomfortable, which motivates us to close it. We can close it by lowering our expectations or raising our performance, but there are other options too. For example, we can imagine having already closed it and then pay more attention to this imagined state than we pay to the real state. Sometimes this can be very useful; for example, when your energy flags in the middle of a long project, pretending that you are closer to the end of it than you really are can give yourself an energy boost. It may not be honest but it can be useful. It may set you up for a letdown later when you remember that completion is a ways off, but later, you may have more enthusiasm and be able to take the disappointment.

Maintaining optimistic delusion requires fudging the books, turning a blind eye to evidence of how one is really doing. In small doses, fudging isn't a problem, but it can become a problem if sustained for prolonged periods. One can get addicted to overly hopeful gap-readings, and end up corrupting one's ability to take reality checks. The longer we spend focusing on optimistic illusions, the bigger the disappointment becomes when we have to step back in and face reality. "He's a legend in his own mind," his friends say behind his back, and if they confront him about his delusional thinking, he's got inoculant at the ready to neutralize his friend' feedback.

Dashed expectations can make us wonder about our ability to plan and about the virtues of planning at all. Maybe you should be more flexible, take it as it comes, see what opportunities arise. While they say that if you don't know where you're going, you'll end up somewhere else, even if you do know where you are going, you can end up somewhere else, or worse, end up where you intended to be but with little interest in being there.

Sometimes it seems we'd be better off without this mind's eye monitoring system. Athletes perform their best when they aren't distracted with worries about how they are performing. Maybe there's a way of life in no expectations.

Dashed expectations can make us wonder about our ability to plan and about the virtues of planning at all. Maybe you should be more flexible, take it as it comes, see what opportunities arise. While they say that if you don't know where you're going, you'll end up somewhere else, even if you do know where you are going, you can end up somewhere else, or worse, end up where you intended to be but with little interest in being there.

Change Plans vs. Change Expectations

How it shows up:

If X, then change plans.

If Y, then change expectations.

Getting it wrong:

False positive: Abandoning plans when relaxing expectations would be better.

False negative: Relaxing expectations when changing plans would be better.

Too sure: Not questioning your plans or expectations when it would be useful to do so.

Too unsure: Questioning your plans and expectations when you needn't.

Whirrings at Night:

We should be in the black by now. Maybe it's time to change tactics, or maybe we were just a little too optimistic.

Why didn't I see this coming? I must have been living a dream.

Why can't we change course. When an option like this comes along shouldn't we be more open-minded?

What they'll call you, if you:

	Change Plans	**Change expectations**
Prove Right	Flexible Agile Adaptive	Dogged Focused Indomitable
Prove Wrong	Flaky Unpredictable Undisciplined	Rigid Close-minded Stuck

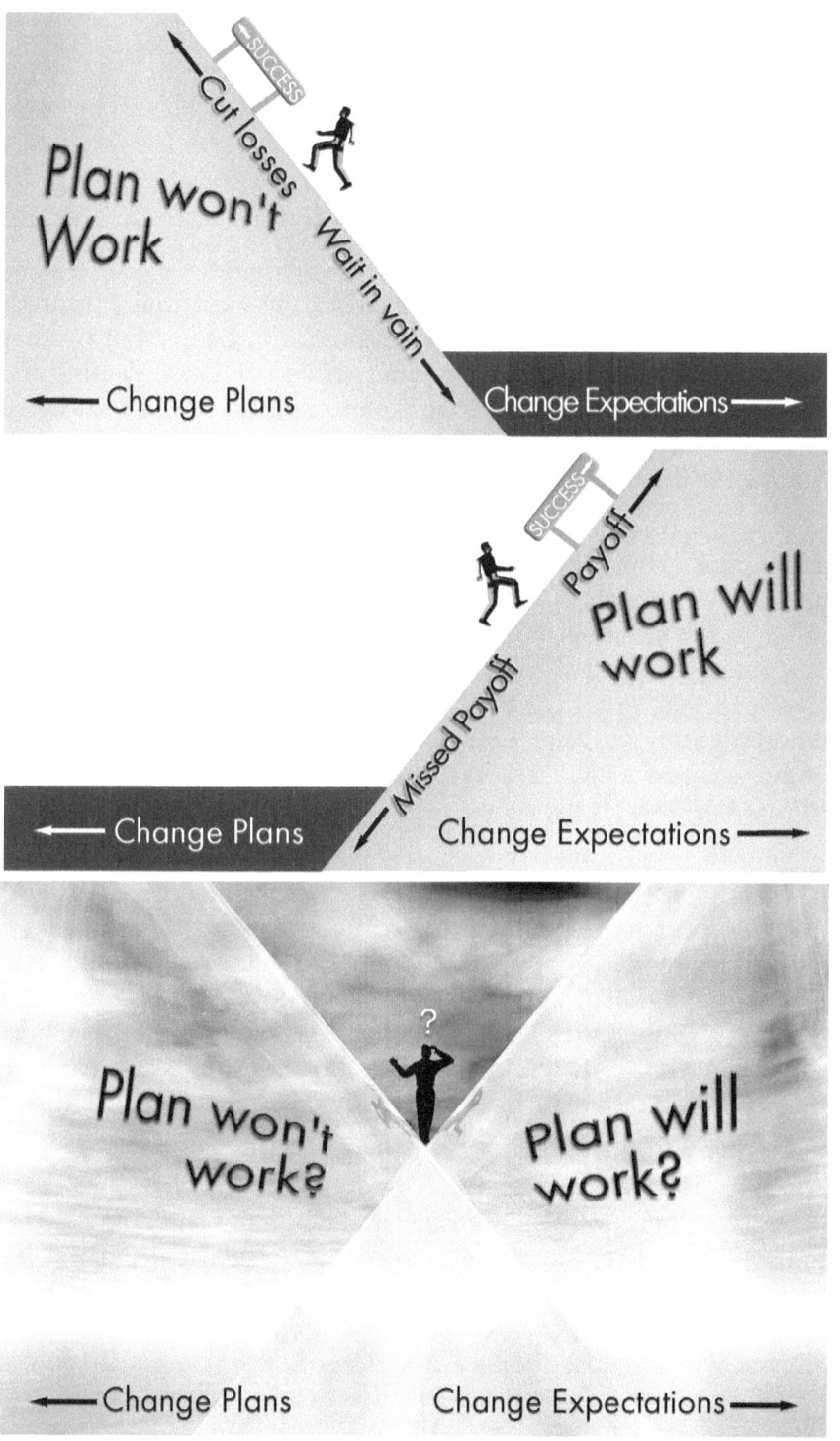

Just fork-edit:

"You can't predict the future"

"Just be here now"

To calm a wondering mind, "be here now" can be a useful mantra, but as a way of life, it is better suited to potato bugs.

Unlike potato bugs, we build our worldview gradually through experience. Our memories are stocks of impressions that we mix and match looking for cues to what will work next. Visiting the past is useful to our efforts to make our futures here and now be good ones. You can't help but have plans and expectations. They come with the territory of being human instead of a potato bug.

And it's true that you can't predict the future with absolute accuracy, but that's never really been the point. On the outcomes you can control, you want to employ what control you can in order to do the most with what you're dealt and to achieve the outcomes you prefer. What does predict mean anyway? If you take it to mean presage the future, no, we are not omniscient or omnipotent. If you take it instead as a term for the human activity of guessing what will become, then of course we can predict the future. We do it all the time.

Sooner or later, every one of us encounters evidence that on the really crucial matters like health, we can't control as much as we'd like to. Aging, for example, is like a sticky fuel indicator on a long road trip. We glance at it occasionally as we travel through early life, knowing that at the rate we are going the tank will eventually get empty. Sometimes it seems to hover in one place for a while, so we ignore it. But then it starts to move and one day we look down and see that it's reading far lower than we expected. An unexpected health leak and the gauge may plummet to empty in no time.

No, we can't control everything, and while some people attempt to use this as a reason to get fatalistic, it doesn't really work. It's flawed logic to interpret the fact that we can't control everything as evidence that we can't control anything, and the main reason anyone would subscribe to a doctrine of foregone conclusion is as a way to persuade oneself to either relax expectations or stop the mind's endless whirring debate over plans, expectations, and goals. It's an absolute that might help reduce an obsession with the future, but it will never work absolutely. Though we never can tell, we live and die trying to tell.

Take It Personally (T.I.P.)
When suffering, adopt a mascot.

Be here now is a kind of nostalgia for pre-human mind. Our pets get to be here now. Having little or no capacity to make human-style mental movies, they have nowhere to be but here and now.

No doubt a cat hit by a car feels pain. Its mind may screech a very severe form of "Ouch!" as loud and as authentic as the ouch you would feel. But a cat does not spend much time on why its leg is broken, delving into the past for an explanation the way you would, or formulating plans for recovery or retribution. The cat is in the here and now. No place else to be.

On a stressful day their calm acceptance of "what is" looks enviable. It's OK to envy an animal its simplicity, but face it, you're not quite like them.

Pain of any sort, psychological or physical, makes us yearn for an explanation and a plan to avoid it in the future, but there's a catch: The more we yearn to make it right, the more bias we bring to our analysis. When we're burning to know why something happened, we are usually burning to find out that the explanation is of one kind and not another, for example not our fault (the tyrannical "why me?" question). So paradoxically, the more desperately we need to know why, the less likely we are to be able to find out. As some Buddhists say, "Truth waits for eyes unclouded by desire" —especially the desperate desire to discover that it's the kind of truth we're hoping it is and not some other more disappointing kind.

When we humans find ourselves in pain, we often forget to say "Ouch!" and beeline instead to an investigation of the pain's origins, an analysis of the perpetrator (as though there always is one), and plan for how to fix it.

It's handy to have patience, taking time to just say "Ouch," for a little while, and postpone all decision making and planning until the biases subside. One way to do this is to adopt a mascot.

When you are hurting, picture yourself hurting like a suffering animal. Pick any one—for example a dog with a broken leg. It lies there in pain, perhaps whining its equivalent of ouch. But it doesn't lurch to explanation, because it can't.

But go easy on yourself if being dog-like doesn't come easy. We are, after all not just any dogs. We're seeing-I dogs. When we're down we see ourselves in pain, and so sputtering, "I wish . . . " and "I've been assaulted . . . " and "From now on, I'm going to . . . " comes much easier to us.

The Third Wondering of the Modern World:

Can This Person Change?

Your mind's eye fills with movies of people, and why they do what they do.

Why do we care what's up with other people? In large part because we want the wisdom to know not only what in our environment we can change, but whom.

Can you get your kid, friend, boss, employee, lover, spouse, or self to do what you hope they'll do or to stop doing what you wish they wouldn't? When you've tried everything you can think of and it hasn't worked, you are likely to wonder whether they can't or just won't. *"He says he's trying (he's very trying), but I'm not sure he knows what trying is. Still, maybe it's the best he can do."* You run different scenarios through your mind's eye trial-and-error process looking for the interpretation that fits best—making movies of yourself saying and doing different things, and then imagining his response. As a mental movie director, you need to understand your actor's motives. It matters because *can't* and *won't* suggest diametrically opposed solutions. If he simply can't do what you'd like him to do, then you wouldn't want to waste your time trying to get him to change. Instead you'd want find some work-around solution or maybe leave—either decorate the pillar in the middle of your living room that the carpenter says you can't remove, or move to a different house.

But if with a little more effort, he could change, then the last thing you want to do is accommodate or leave. Instead, you'd want to encourage, provoke, push, and pull—do whatever it takes to stimulate the change.

Troubled marriages steep in this dilemma. Troubled children are the subjects of endless speculation. Troublesome bosses and employees, politicians and criminals—when they tick us off we can't help but wonder what makes them tick, largely to enable us to figure out what if anything we can do to change them. Don't accommodate the indulgent or you're codependent. Do accommodate the handicapped or you are callous. This is easy advice to follow so long as it's clear who's indulgent and who's handicapped. If that isn't clear, then it's maddeningly difficult advice to follow.

Human behavior is driven by the complex interactions of biological, emotional, intellectual, and cultural guidance. It is much harder to read and interpret the behavior of humans than the other elements of our immediate environment. Since humans are such a significant part of our environment, we have accumulated a lot of specialized adaptive guidance for reading our fellow human's motives. This guidance is such a significant part of our tool kit that we tend to rely upon it when interpreting the behavior of nonhuman elements of our environment too. If your handiest tool is a hammer, everything looks like a nail. If your handiest capacity is the ability to read minds and intentions, everything appears to have minds and intentions to read. We readily imagine our computers, pets, houseplants, cars—even Mother Nature—as though they had minds of their own, very much like ours. A lot of what has driven this over-generalized mind-reading capacity is the pressing need to know who around us can be bent to our purposes, and who can bend us toward theirs.

All questions of justice are inextricably linked to this concern also. Does the perpetrator of a crime belong in jail or a mental institution? We don't want to jail the mentally ill. They can't help how they are. We do want to jail the criminal because he or she can help it, but won't.

Some say you should never punish people who can't help themselves because punishing them won't help. Others say that punishment is more than just a teaching aid for the perpetrators of crimes. It's a deterrent to those who might be tempted to commit similar crimes but could help it. Maybe punishing people isn't strategic at all but rather the eye-for-eye retaliation we can't help but make when someone hurts us. "Why," they say, "should we make allowances for people who can't help but commit crimes and not make allowances for ourselves when we can't help but punish them?"

Wondering what we can and can't change within ourselves is the topic of some of our liveliest inner debates and negotiations. In advance, we wonder, will we pass the test and, if not, is our failure because we didn't try hard enough or because we just don't have the talent it takes? In retrospect, we wonder whether we couldn't help our mistakes, or could have we had tried harder. To say, "Hey, I'm trying," doesn't resolve the question. Everyone is trying. The question is, how much? Eighty percent? One hundred and ten percent? There's bound to be uncertainty.

You may be the last person you can reasonably ask to assess your own effort, because you care so much and therefore bring biases to the question. We don't want to think of ourselves as lazy or limited. Calling ourselves fundamentally limited closes the gap once and for all, which would be a relief if it weren't also the end of aspiration to improve.

At least if it's a fundamental limitation, it's not our fault. By calling alcoholism a disease, the alcoholic is free from blame. Today scientists are discovering that many afflictions formerly attributed to indulgence have underlying biochemical causes. These discoveries trouble us, because we suspect that people will use them self-servingly as arguments for complacency. In describing troubles, we smuggle in implied prognoses for change under the safe cover of unexamined analogies. In describing our work on a personal problem as "healing old wounds," we imply that the problem was imposed from the outside that will disappear with treatment. Scars don't disappear. Phases do. Our crosscutting biases aren't self-canceling; they tug at us antagonistically making our self-assessments somewhat suspect.

So why not rely on outsider's assessment of how much we're trying? First, outsiders bring biases to the question too, but more importantly, they have no way of knowing how much effort we're making compared to what we can. Since our nerve endings don't extend into each other's bodies we have no way to compare one person's efforts to another's, only their performance.

Take weight-gain. People who carry extra pounds endure disapproving looks from people whose snap assessment is that fat is evidence of weak-willed indulgence. And is it? Maybe, but not necessarily. Three variables determine weight gain and willpower to eat less and exercising more is only one of them. Appetite for exercise and food is a second variable: Two people with equal willpower will gain differently if their fundamental desire for food and exercise are different. The third variable is metabolism. Two people leading equally active lives and eating equal amounts will carry weight differently. Three variables and no way for the casual onlooker to assess which ones are at work.

And weight is just an example. We all make assessments of each other's capacity to change and we all endure each other's assessments.

One form that this wonder takes in modern life is ambiguity about how to measure each other's merit. We measure merit both by effort and by performance. Do we care whether the criminal is trying hard or just whether he broke the law? Do we retain a nonperforming employee because he is really, reeeeally trying? Are we drawn to physically attractive people or people who make the most effort to be physically attractive? Do we make friends with people who perform well by our standards or who try hardest? Of course, effort and performance are correlated. In general the harder one tries, the better one does, but across populations this doesn't work. We are born with different talents and into different circumstances. Equal effort must overcome unequal obstacles.

Take lookism in general: In a world that seems to be making some progress on racism, lookism remains one of the most widespread remaining biases. It is also one of the most taboo. It biases the allocation of power within corporations, but you won't see lookism diversity workshops any time soon.

For fair-minded folks, it's troubling that overweight and homely people should fare less well than fit and handsome people. But what can we do about it? Blame our culture, which certainly amplifies it, but the unfair allocation of resources and opportunities is as old as life itself. Blame ourselves for it? Not if we can help it. Blame the disadvantaged? Unconsciously, most of us do at one time or another, because it resolves the dissonance we feel between measuring merit by performance and by effort. If they aren't trying hard enough to lose weight or meet any other given performance standard then it's not our problem; the world is fair and they aren't taking advantage of their equal opportunity.

Biological life measures merit by performance only, which is one of the main reasons people resist evolutionary theory. Mother Nature has no sympathy for underachievers. In her great sifting she purges those that don't meet the performance standard. And her nonhuman creatures are as ruthless as she.

No lion cuts the laggard lamb slack for trying harder to escape. Not even a mother bird can afford to invest more in her runt than in her strongest baby. Inequality is intrinsic to the trial and error process. Of course, in nature sometimes the underdog wins. We can take comfort in knowing that you never can tell which trials will prove successful. Still, there's no denying that some things do and some things don't succeed. It's true that we are all born with different appetites and aptitudes, but untrue that each of us has a special gift of equal value. At best this comforting myth enables us to forestall awareness of the obvious for a few years with impressionable children rather than see them humiliated by one another's ruthless performance standards.

The unfairness of selection is one of the most unappealing facts of life, but only to us humans. It's only through the human capacity to imagine a world of fully fair distribution that we begin to aspire to transcend the nonhuman world's inequality. By way of mental movie making we can put ourselves in each other's shoes, experience empathy, and imagine ultimate fairness for all. The male elk whose subordinate status prevents him from mating must experience great frustration, but he can't probably feel bitterness, humiliation, or the impulse to strive for equality, because he has no way to maintain a mental image of himself living in a fairer world.

It's the mind's eye that makes us so altruistic. We can't help but picture our fellow creatures and the collective good, more so than can other living beings. It is true that ants are more collective than us. But their collectivity is different from ours; it is closer to the altruism of exchange that goes on between your heart and your lungs. It's not a matter of choice but of evolved necessity. We humans choose whether to care for each other or not. Having a mental image of our species—something no other species members have had before—we can feel the impulse to love humankind, and then are forever burdened with the question, how much?

Limited vs. Lazy

How it shows up:
If he is limited then do plan A.

If he is lazy then plan B.

Getting it wrong:
False positive: Reading laziness as limit.

False negative: Reading limit as laziness.

Too sure: Assuming you know which it is, when you don't.

Too unsure: Wondering whether you know, when you do.

Whirrings at Night:
Does he mean to treat me this way?

Does she realize what she's doing?

Is he trying to ignore me?

Is it her fault that her looks are fading, but then again is it my fault that I'm no longer attracted to her?

Have I tried hard enough?

Am I making excuses for myself?

Could he have been saved?

What they'll call you, if you:

	Guess limited	Guess lazy
Prove Right	Compassionate Sensitive Realistic	Tough-minded No push-over Demanding
Prove Wrong	Naïve Too accommodating Low standards	Uncompassionate Mean Ungenerous

Just fork-edit:

'You can't change others; only yourself'

'Never give up on someone'

The world in which no creature changes any other creature would be very different from this one. Since the lion's share of any creature's environment is other creatures, evolution has built into all creatures the capacity to influence each other's behavior. From the mating dance to the parasitic takeover, behavior is largely about the extension of one body's influence over another. What better way to leverage our finite energy than to use it to press another creature's energy into service on our behalf?

With human power of symbolic communication and mental movie making, the power of persuasion escalates. We can influence each other's mental movies, programming and reprogramming each other at a phenomenal pace. It may sound like dark science fiction but it's both a boon and a bane. Human organizations are only as strong as the alignment their members share around commonly held mental movies. We wouldn't have the collective power to do good if people couldn't be persuaded to climb on the bandwagon of the shared vision. And this capacity is also the power to do collective evil.

We humans not only evolve tools of persuasion, we also co-evolve tools for resisting persuasion. To resist change, we have a have a full spectrum of antibodies—from mild to strong. We can resist each other's influence either on substantive grounds or through blanket close-mindedness. Consider this continuum:

"Thanks, but sorry, I'm not interested. I'm on a different path."

"Sorry, I've found a better path than the one you're offering."

"Your path is fundamentally wrong."

"People on your path should be put in jail."

"Death to those on a path other than mine."

At the extreme, zealots have strong antibodies to infection by others intent on changing their behavior—so strong that they cross over into changing other people's behavior, including terrorizing those who do not share their beliefs. Zealots unwittingly cross the line into imposition on others through a kind of internal shadowboxing, an attempt to shout down internalized influences. We say what we feel the need to hear. And if we need to hear something loud enough to overpower something else we're hearing, we shout.

Persuasive extension runs deep and old as life. It's life's master currency. The absolutist argument that you can't change anyone makes sense therefore primarily as something we say when we need to hear the chant of acceptance, serenity, and resignation about someone we tried to change but have decided we can't, or else it's something we can say to get ourselves to stop wondering whether we can or can't change a certain someone.

And its opposite—that you should never give up on someone— is used similarly. It too is not absolutely true. The benefits of maintaining an investment in hope would be absolute, were it not that hope entails some cost. Hope is an investment in a goal and expectation, it focuses your finite attention on something-- something that might or might not be a good investment of your use attention. To never give up on someone changing in ways you hope they will translates into practical decisions that are tantamount to holding out some prospect that they will change, and while you can remain optimistic in principle you do have to allocate your finite energy carefully and don't want to hold out for things that won't happen.

You can and can't change people; you should and shouldn't try. The lifelong conundrum is figuring out how and who and in what circumstances.

Take It Personally (T.I.P.)

I may not be able to change myself, but I can probably change my environment so that it changes me.

We are very much creatures of our environment, and our environment is mostly comprised of other people. If in Darwin's first interpretation of the evolutionary process, adaptation happens when traits are filtered through the natural selection imposed by environmental conditions and our human environment consists primarily of other people, then people are for us a form of selective filtering. And of course they are. Try out a behavior on someone and if it's greeted with a frown, that frown "selects" on your behavior, either encouraging or discouraging it depending upon whether that person is someone you systematically defer to or defy.

Now if you believe that there is such a thing as a true core self, wholly independent of what other people think and how they react, then this notion that who we are is largely comprised of other people's influences on us is bad news. But if you can accept it, you can use it to your advantage. To the extent that you can choose the company you keep, you can selectively exploit people's influence over you as a way to change yourself in ways you'd like to change.

The selective sifting that matters to you most from day to day is the sifting that comes from exposure to other people. So notice first what they sift for. When people wince when you say something, that's a filter, sifting through your options of what to say and discouraging you from saying anything like that again. Obversely, their smile encourages you to say more of the same or similar things.

Do you like how they are filtering you? That is, do you surround yourself with people who bring out your best and grow you in the directions that you want to grow?

If not, do what you can to replace them with people who do. Your peers shape you. You have nothing to mirror but peers themselves.

Become a selectrician, selecting what filters you subject yourself to—wiring up your friendships and associations (to the extent that you have control) so that they grow you in the directions you'd like to grow.

This applies especially to dating and mating. The more attractive your mate is, the more powerful his or her sifting effect will be upon you. Therefore be as careful as you can be about whom you bring into your life at such close range. The attractive ones are the most dangerous because they are your strongest selective filters. It matters a lot that their ideas of who you can be are compatible with yours. Their perception of your becomes the physical world embodiment of your goals—the aspiration of your aspirational gap. Attractive and compatible, not just attractive—that's what you're looking for.

Attractiveness alone was good enough when you were young and had no idea what you wanted to become. First love is like climbing onto an express train headed lord knows where. Its destination didn't matter so long as the ride was fast and exciting. To the extent that you have become discerning about who you are and what you become, it is no longer enough. Therefore you want to pick people who are compatible company and perhaps the most important compatibility is in your styles of negotiating your inevitable incompatibilities. In first love many of us rush headlong into each other singing, "all of me, why not take all of me?" If you were lucky enough to experience the full train-wreck of first love, you and your soul mate for life fed each other so well for a time that complete merging seemed possible, and then you learned. You have to be careful what you surrender too. Later love at its best knows better than to let the other person in on all levels and in all ways. We may still long for the purity of the full merger, but most of us know better than to surrender ourselves full to one person's selective filtering.

By mid-life love becomes the negotiation between two people who want to merge and want space as well, which means that with each other we must wonder what to try to change and what to let be, what to allow them to change in you and what to hold independently. There's more room for misunderstanding and rejection in this. One night you want your partner and your partner wants space. Or vice versa. Compatibility in negotiating the compatibility means finding a partner who understands this more complex dance in the same way you do. So that though there will be the misunderstanding, there is an abiding appreciation of the fact that there is benefit to noticing which tentacles of selectivity to invite and which ones to pass up in each other's company.

The Fourth Wondering of the Modern World:

Should I Look at This?

When any wondering persists in a disturbing way you'll wonder whether you are better off trying to decrease or increase the attention that you give to it. Face it or ignore it? Broach it with others or keep it to yourself? That's the fourth wondering of the modern world. Remember the wondering of the ancient world, "Is this a cue?" "Should I look at this?" is an internal equivalent, a mental moviemaker's question about what to show on your internal screen—not that any of us have anywhere near complete control over what we think about, but we get some say in the matter. We also have the capacity to selectively blurt, not saying everything that comes to mind. The question becomes whether playing the disturbing scene in your mind's eye and by extension declaring it to others helps you work through it or only mires you deeper in it.

We've got aphorisms, analogies, and allegory galore for dealing with this one, but they weigh in on both sides of it, leaving us to wonder what we should do.

The truth will set you free. Shout it out of your system. To name it is to tame it. Confront your demons; tell it like it is; the emperor has no clothes. Once you declare what's eating you, it loses its appetite; if you share your burden with others, they can help lighten the load; they'll suggest things you can do about it, or at least comfort you through empathy and news that they too have had similar burdens. Confront a bully. If you don't you'll never hear the end of it. Taking action with a persistent problem is like putting a wet towel out in the sunlight where it will dry out before mildewing.

Or maybe airing your problem is like airing your dirty laundry, opening a can of worms or chanting "I'm angry" until you're furious. It only amplifies it. Maybe you're better off keeping it to yourself, or better still ignoring it altogether. Why worry? Don't you realize that most of the things you worry about take care of themselves eventually? If you don't put your attention on it, it will go away. Ignore a bully and he'll lose interest. Airing a burning issue only feeds the flame.

But leaving a smoldering ember lying around is dangerous too. It may sear right through you before you know it. Leave a wound unattended and it will fester. You have to treat a wound in order to heal it.

This is not nearly the issue for our fellow creatures that it is for us. We share with other mammals a capacity to toggle between a calm base state generated by the parasympathetic nervous system and a state of heightened alertness to danger generated by the sympathetic nervous system. For other mammals it toggles pretty efficiently—calm when safe, alert in danger—but for us the toggling is much more messy because even when safe we can rerun mental movie footage of past experiences of danger and imaginable future dangers. We alone can freak ourselves out.

The foreboding signs of possible problems are sometimes false alarms to ignore if you can, but sometimes they're worth heeding. Think of all the amazing precautionary, preventative, and protective systems and organizations we have developed because we have this marvelous capacity to read and attend to early warnings. Other creatures don't invent new kinds of danger the way we humans do, but they also have far less capacity to innovate in response to them either.

Our mental movie making capacity has primed us to find virtual reality remarkably credible. We feel the sensations of present danger—real bodily agitation—whether we are experiencing a nightmare, a terrible thought, a ghost story, or a blockbuster horror film. And terror is intrinsically vivid. An implausible but catastrophic scenario can seem plausible simply because it's so vivid. It's as though we've got an adaptive bias toward exaggerating the worst that could happen, because it is safer to err on the side of caution. At the same time we are highly motivated to eliminate the danger, or at least the fear. We are therefore tugged in two directions at once. Nothing snaps our heads to attention like terror, and we are at great pains to dispel the fear. Sometimes we get the worst of both worlds, finding ways of dispelling the fear without dispelling the danger.

The simple solution would be to put your attention only on the things that are going to cause you trouble and never think about the things that won't, and likewise only give voice to the things that will benefit from exposure but never to the things that

159

won't. But doing that would not only require extraordinary will power and discipline that would enable you to turn stress on and off at will, it would also take the wisdom to know the difference between what is worth sweating and what isn't.

So there are times when we're stressed and we needn't be, our attention riveted on some imagined danger that doesn't deserve it or lingering on a danger that has long since past. We realize this, and so wondering about whether to pay attention to something takes on a strategic relevance. If you've got some trouble loitering in your mind longer than you think is useful, and you're trying to figure out how to flush it out, you have the choice between trying to purge it by expelling it into the limelight or by containing and digesting it. Either approach might succeed and either approach might backfire.

Address vs. Ignore

How it shows up:

If cue A then address.

If cue B then ignore.

Getting it wrong:

False positive: Addressing a problem in ways that amplify it.

False negative: Ignoring a problem in ways that make it smolder and burn.

Too sure: Not even considering whether to address to or ignore it when considering the option would help you chose the approach that would work best.

Too unsure: Wondering whether to address or ignore when you are already doing the right thing.

Whirrings at Night:

Is it time to face this?

Maybe I need help.

This has gone on too long; it's time to do something about it.

I should just forget about this and get some rest. By tomorrow morning it will all look completely different.

Why am I always so quick to jump to the worst-case scenario?

What they'll call you, if you:

	Address it	Ignore it
Prove Right	Brave Unflinching Alert	Practical A good prioritizer Relaxed
Prove Wrong	Fussy Negative Meddlesom	In denial Closed Defensive

Just fork-edit:

'Don't be in denial'
'Don't be negative''

Between these two absolutes, you can't win. Not facing disappointing news is denial, but facing it is negative. And actually both the terms *denial* and *negative* are negative, which is not to say that either the act of being "in denial," or the act of being "negative" are intrinsically wrong, but rather that whoever calls those acts by these names is using pejorative terms as a way to discourage you from taking these acts. Negative or positive spin aside, these terms simply refer to two generic strategic moves we can make when it comes to discouraging cues that persist. We can either put our attention on it or not put our attention on it.

The underlying problem that makes us wonder which to do is guesscrow—that annoying catch 22 mentioned above. The world won't release its escrow account of support for your bet until you place it. It won't even let you know how much is in the account until you place it. But that makes it hard to place the bet. When this wonder comes up it's because the cues are ambiguous: You can't tell whether you are in a situation that will improve only when you intervene, or only when you let things run their natural course.

Try this scenario: You're married and you and your partner are both committed for the long haul. Being human, you both recognize that enthusiastic commitment for a marriage waxes and wanes with moods. Further, you recognize that a relationship is a feedback loop with ripples of either deeper commitment or greater distance reverberating dialectically. *A* causes *B* while *B* causes *A*: That is, your attitude can change your spouse's, which in turn can change yours. Which means that every time one of you declares that the passion isn't present, it can make the other feel like pulling back.

Suppose then, that one day your spouse happens to be feeling the love and you aren't particularly. To avoid being in denial on this important matter, you say, "I need you to know that today I'm not feeling much love. Today, I'm bored and find myself dreaming of alternatives to spending the rest of my life with you." No one likes their love to go unreciprocated at such close range, so naturally, this makes your spouse recoil which in turn can make you pull back. So maybe keeping your momentary reaction to yourself isn't so bad. Denial at this level can be a good thing. Throw yourself all the way into your commitment and that way the world and your spouse above all will release more of the escrow of support that will make the commitment pay off. After all, you don't want to be negative.

Which then raises the question: If your lack of enthusiasm persists, how long should you deny it? At what point are you doing your spouse a disservice by not mentioning it?

"I'm not happy and actually I haven't been for several years now."

Would you have been better off being negative earlier? It's not very clear what people mean when they say, "Don't be negative." They are certainly discouraging something, but what are they discouraging? Pessimism of any sort? Where's the line between saying that things are not going well enough to continue them without alteration and the kind of dissatisfaction we call negative?

It's not just with spouses but with all persistent problems, businesses in the red longer than expected, markets slumping; when is declaring a cash flow problem worth the damage to employee morale?

A remarkable number of people operate on the assumption that we have the power to make something bad happen simply by saying that it could, but the opposite is as true. By not attending to a warning flag that an important fork may be coming up, we are often caught unprepared and miss an opportunity to avert the problem.

There's a temperamental component to the fourth wondering. At one end of a continuum are people who can't help but blurt their thoughts out about any- and everything that bugs them. They take up a lot of space. Their anxieties read like an open book, and if you suggest that they shut the book, they act like there is some moral imperative to speak the truth. And at the other end of the continuum are the nonstop stoics, who on principle won't confront. Most of us are in between, with a proclivity toward either pole, but enough ambivalence to wonder in certain situations which option would be better.

164

Take It Personally (T.I.P.)

Life is experienced in color but often must be lived in black and white.

In the push and pull of galactic psychology, waves of doubt streak through the atmosphere of our thoughts and feelings like meteorites. They pass through at odd angles, shifting our center of gravity before burning out or passing on. The atmosphere is thick with reasons to shift one way, the other, or both, and therefore our emotional and mental lives are complex. But we need to keep things simple, mustering some degree of constancy or other people in our social galaxy won't know how to deal with us. Taking a stand is often nothing more than averaging our disparate feelings and learning to neutralize the fluctuations.

Take a moment to consider your givens—the positions you have to hold constant for public consumption: where you work, who you live with, what you are to your dependents, how you hold the story of your past so that you can declare what you've learned from it rather than reliving and rethinking it always. The world sifts your behavior for specific behaviors but it also sifts for simple constancy. To get by, act one way, even if you shake and toggle many ways on the inside. A Zen saying captures it well: "Though my heart is on fire my eyes are cold as ashes." While the body experiences fluctuations between hot and cold; society demands that you maintain warmth—not too hot; not too cold.

What we each choose to attend to or ignore, declare or conceal, is certainly a function of temperament, but also of circumstance. Some of us are under much more pressure to tell consistent stories than others. A surgeon needs a steady hand; a soldier to do or die; a banker to appear as reliable as the marble building in which she works, but a rock star, painter, or writer is rewarded for giving voice to the subtleties of human emotion. At the end of the workday our appetites are different too. Some of us seek balance—a chance to loosen up after a day of professional stoicism. Others can't afford to relax because it would take so much effort to button up again for work. Notice your style and circumstances and the ways in which they are compatible and incompatible with the people whose company you keep. Many of us suffer from "be-like-me" syndrome—a sense that our way is the appropriate way or at least a reliance on arguments that defend our way even at the expense of offending people with other approaches. Being compatible in negotiating incompatibilities means recognizing the fundamental tension created by the fact that life is experienced across a spectrum of emotional shadings but must often be lived in black and white. Recognizing this enables us to appreciate the different compromises people come up with in order to maintain of degree of equanimity in spite of it. Stoic people aren't necessarily unimaginative. Different people; different circumstances. As with the weight gain question, we can't necessarily tell what makes people tick. Sure, some people are more disciplined than others, but we also have different appetites for mood swings, and different capacities for digesting them.

And notice too, the macro trends that shape the supply of and demand for simple button-down stories. The service economy, the advent of jumbo corporate capitalism, and the expectation of ever-accelerating productivity are upping the demand for reliable workers, while cultural diversity is eroding the power of uniform belief. Five hundred years ago people and ideas didn't travel far, we weren't reared to apply critical thinking, and almost nothing of what was successful in the world had succeeded through the disciplined application of the kind of doubt and skepticism that our culture now celebrates. It was easier to know what to think, believe, and say and what to ignore, deny, and shun. Now, with cultural diversity and the weakening of our formal institutional standard-bearing religions, it's much harder to know when to keep your mind and mouth shut and when to think and speak up. With old wisdom no longer as applicable, we are fourth-wondering more than ever.

The Fifth Wondering of the Modern World:

Should I Be More Realistic?

Living both in an inner and an outer world, we face a tough choice about how much to attend to each. Why not seek perfect harmony between the two? Make your inner world accurately reflect your outer one. Only play documentaries, not fiction, in your mind's eye movie theater. Be a realist. Most of us think we are. Our mental movies feel vividly realistic and we believe them, so they must be realistic, right . . . ?

Well anyway, who says it's best to be a realist? If you dream up a better world than the real one, you can help make it a reality. The first step is seeing the world as the world is not, even though that's unrealistic.

Be a realist or a dreamer? This is the fifth wondering of the modern world—another peculiarly human wondering since we're the creatures with the lively inner world that competes with the outer one for our attention.

Setting aside for a moment the advantages and disadvantages of wishful thinking or envisioning better futures, let's revisit a question that came up in the natural history of doubt.

The mind's eye sifts through a lot of movie footage—memories, theories, scenarios, stories: ideas, basically—and selectively retains some for more frequent replay than others. What are the mind's selection standards? Sure, it selects for realism, but that is not the only or even the most important criterion.

The mind selects ideas that sit well or fit snugly with several different contexts, of which the real physical world we call reality is only one. Another is our cultural context, which includes the general zeitgeist of our times, but most directly the people whose approval and disapproval we monitor. Even the most independent thinkers among us choose ideas that conform to social conventions, which we know from history can be a little unrealistic. The business maverick who breaks away from the pack does so in noticeable but narrow ways, not breaking from all cultural norms, but rather a select few. We may lionize the maverick as someone who "breaks all the rules," but we don't mean it. It's breaking the right ones that counts.

167

Another critical context is our existing constellation of already retained ideas: It's easier to hold a thought that is consistent with what we already know and believe than to retain one that is at odds with our existing assumptions. Applied to the ideas that are already floating around in our heads, this standard translates as a kind of check on internal consistency. We feel funny when confronted by inconsistency not just because it bugs other people, but because it bugs us.

Another context is our form—what we're dealt, the constraints of our capacities described in the seventh wondering of the ancient world. Mental limitations, for example. We are more likely to retain an idea that we readily understand than an idea that we find difficult and complex even if the more difficult and complex idea is truer. Our form includes all the proclivities we're born with. We tend to prefer ideas that affirm our natural temperaments and appetites.

Another context is habit: We are more likely to retain an idea we use every day than one we don't ever use. Many of us, for example, forget the math we haven't used in a long time but remember the ideas we apply every day at work.

Another context is utility. The more an idea pays off, the more likely it is to be a keeper. 'Twas ever thus, with Mother Nature filtering first and foremost for utility. But with mind's eyes too, utility still counts. A farmer can water his fields as a tribute to the Corn God, and regardless of whether there is a Corn God, if the corn grows, the idea of a Corn God grows too.

And then there's what feels good, which in a way is its own context within which our ideas must fit and in another way is the universal indicator by which we measure all of the other kinds of fit. We are more likely to hold ideas that engender strong emotion than thoughts that don't generate much emotion, and we are generally looking for ideas that feel strongly good over ideas that feel strongly bad.

So sure, the mind selects for things that pass reality checks, but there is more than one kind of reality we check with. We could say that there are several inner reality checks—what conforms to our existing mind-set, what feels good, what fits with our mind's capabilities—; and several external ones—what conforms to culture's interpretation of reality and yes, of course, real physical consequence.

But this gets confusing too, because where does your sense of cultural standards reside? In the outside world surely, but also in your mind's eye images of what your culture stands for and in your unconscious internal sense of right and wrong which resides primarily in your emotional response to your own behavior. The mind's selective standards are therefore intertwined, dialectically entangled, which is not the same as cohesively unified. They complement and compete with each other, tugging us in the same direction and in different directions all at once.

This multitude of forces that makes up our minds explains our frequent use of fork-edits like *Persistence furthers*. A doubtful thought sticks to the mind because it makes us scared and scared is a strong emotion. But it doesn't exist in a vacuum. If we're stuck with a scary thought our minds seek an un-scary thought that will make us feel better. If we find one, we are likely to try to hold it. But not in a vacuum. The scary and un-scary thoughts coexist, causing a disquieting inconsistency. One way out is to purge the doubt once and for all. The scarier the doubt; the heavier the doubt-purging artillery we are tempted to employ. A fork-edit is an all-out doubt-purger, the best any of us can muster to put our minds at ease. It's not enough to counter doubt about a project by saying, "it really could work," when you can say, "persistence always furthers." It may not ring very true, but in a practical pinch, a self-affirming absolute is of premium value and we figure out how to ignore its inaccuracy.

We want to make good decisions, but the main way we know whether we have is a feeling—a comfortable sense of confidence we get—a calm bosom and a better night's rest. We can have this feeling faster through self-certainty than through doubt, though doubt might in the long run yield better decisions.

So if the merit of an idea is measured by so many disparate selective standards, why do most of us like to think that we are realists in search of the whole truth and nothing but the truth?

One reason is that the realism is especially popular these days, largely because scientific realism has been so successful. It's not that science has eliminated wishful thinking; it's that our scientific institutions have devised ways to constrain wishful thinking

169

enough that we are getting more of what we wish for than wishful thinking itself provided. About three hundred years ago enlightenment thinkers figured out how to make a paradoxical move that has been very good to us ever since. Newton's revolution, for example, enabled engineers to produce a flurry of hugely adaptive tools that are now indispensable in our toolkit. Newton's method for doing so, built upon the ideas of Francis Bacon, embodied the paradox that to get what we wish for, we have to get beyond what we wish for long enough to see what really is. Guided by the knowledge of what is, we can engineer more effective ways to meet our desires. From Newton forward, science has harnessed realism so successfully that magical thinking has fallen out of favor.

But realism has always been popular as far back as the earliest arguments about what is and isn't true. As long as humans have lived, we can assume paralyzing doubt has made us uncomfortable. It stands to reason then that the ability to claim something as true beyond all shadow of a doubt has always had some appeal. All sorts of things we now know aren't true were valued as true in their time. To this day, think of how many subcultures you've heard about that claim to have found self-evident truths about the real world that you know full well are bogus—wishful thinking dressed up to look like science.

Humankind has a long tradition of assuming that the liked story is also the likely story. And it makes sense that we would, because a story that both feels good and is true is the best of both worlds, the inner and the outer. What could be better than an idea that's easy to think, affirms what we already know, and gains us social approval? An idea that happens by coincidence to be absolutely accurate, endorsed by the laws of physics or nature, the gods above or our intuition. An idea like that would win full consensus support among the judges of our minds trials.

The ultimate magical thinking then is to believe whatever one wants to believe and call it real. What's to stop us? Two things really: the reality check we get from the outside world and our inner reality check for internal consistency.

First, outside world reality checks are stronger on some issues than on others. What is the meaning of life? What is human destiny? What will the future hold? What should big governments do? On issues like these we're not confronted with a lot of real-world data, or what data we get is open to interpretation, and real-world accuracy becomes a less significant criterion than all the rest. On big wide-open questions, we tend to retain and subscribe to ideas that prove useful, feel good, or are affirmed culturally. On other topics upon which facts are much more imposing, accuracy becomes a more significant criterion. For example, many of us rely on self-affirming ideas for our broad and cosmic interpretation of the meaning of life, but most of us rely on scientific methods to determine whether a loved one has cancer.

Second, regarding our inner reality check for internal consistency: Real movie directors hire continuity experts to make sure that the leading man wears the same tie at Tuesday's shoot as he wore last Wednesday when they shot the scene that precedes it. Otherwise there would be inconsistencies from one scene to the next. It's a lot to keep track of, and some movie buffs enjoy hunting down the inconsistencies. How would our mental movies fare in the hands of one of these continuity experts? Most of us talk and act as though we think they'd fair pretty well, as though we each have a cohesive and integrated set of beliefs about reality.

But even if we were dead set on making them cohesive, accurate, and internally consistent, splicing together a cohesive mind-set out of the disparate movie clips we've accumulated would be challenging work because there is no way to play all the movie clips at once and to honestly assess how well they all fit together.

Just as you only sample a small amount of outside reality in any given moment, you only sample a small amount of your internal mind-set at once too. We do our mental movie editing in what's called short-term memory. It's a small space, capable of holding about five to nine film clips at a time. Thinking is like requisitioning a few select scenes from your back lot inventory of footage and splicing them together, perhaps with some new scenes you've just shot.

By the time you've lived as long as you have, you've been doing a lot of requisitioning and splicing, and it would be reasonable to suppose that your whole back lot inventory would be cohesively spliced, well integrated, and satisfactory to a continuity expert.

But with a little motivation in requisitioning footage, any one of us could conveniently avoid bringing together the footage that doesn't fit together well. We could bring to working memory only those pieces that fit together well and avoid bringing in conflicting pieces. And when we encounter a clash we could either set about to figure out which part really belongs or alternatively bring to the table any idea that enables us to dismiss the dissonance. We have the capacity to believe our mind-set is an integrated whole that would meet with the approval of any continuity expert, but all it really takes is a single piece of footage—the simple idea that we have the continuity. Regardless of whether we do or not, one patch—one frequently requisitioned image of the mind as a cohesive whole—becomes a very useful, feel-good idea to keep close at hand.

All of the above argues that we have the capacity to believe things that ain't necessarily so. Now we can return to the question of whether there are benefits in doing so. And there are. Optimism is like the guesscrow commitment that enables the universe to unleash whatever support it might have for your projects. The mind's eye capacity to dreams exposes us to risks of self-delusion, but it is also the source of the human ingenuity and inventiveness. It is by imagining what isn't that we've motivated ourselves to see what is, and through the combination of longing for a better world and seeing the world as it really is we've come this far. Indeed, anyone who thinks science's take-home message is be a realist is taking half the truth and leaving the other half behind. Science isn't realism instead of dreaming; it is the proper harnessing of realism in the service of dreaming. Through science we gained the wisdom to know a little more of the difference between when to dream and when to get real. With our prodigious powers of imagination, humans have the capacity to invent tools of all sorts. One kind of invention that is particularly interesting here is the kind that enables us to trick our feelings, making them think they are getting something that they aren't.

The mind's eye was the world's first form of virtual reality. Thinking itself is this capacity to see in a virtual world what isn't in front of us in the real world. Much of human ingenuity and engineering has gone into the creation of worldly manifestations of the virtual. For example, 30,000 year old cave paintings as virtual horses, 20,000 year old face painting as virtual facial features, coins as virtual resources, numeric symbols as virtual bags of grain—the list goes on to include all forms of fiction and today an explosion of virtual technologies: computer screens as virtual paper on which we can write fiction with spell-checked words casting spells of imagination and showing pornographic pixilations as virtual sex; fat-free fat and sugar-free sugar; video games as virtual adventure; make-up, photo touch-up, and breast implants as virtual youth; Viagra as virtual vitality; musical instruments that play themselves; an endless array of ways to meet performance standards virtually, with a fraction of the effort of meeting them really.

Watch the wonderful ways these inventions play out. We like sugar because it tastes sweet, but why does it taste sweet? Originally, because the feeling of pleasure we derived from eating fruit that was good for our survival and therefore our reproductive success. A sweet tooth like a lust for fatty foods guided and motivated us to find food that was hard to come by but made a big difference to our energy, survival, and biological reproductive success. As such, a sweet tooth was a tool that passed through Mother Nature's sieve.

And what do you get when you cross a desire for sugar with the capacity to make mental movies? A capacity to imagine and pursue ultimate satisfaction—Mr. Goodbar, in this case, a confection. We have the ingenuity to turn our dreams of ultimate satisfaction into improvements upon reality and we have focused it on the ultimate satisfaction of our sweet teeth: the sugar cane industry, taffy pulling machines, cocoa plantations, fruit-flavored gummy worms, and convenience stores that no longer carry fruit, just seed-free fruit-flavored goodies.

We now find nutrition-free candy and soft drinks anywhere we turn. They satisfy the heck out of our sweet teeth but don't, in fact, supply us with the nutrients that the sweet tooth used to guide us to. This may sound like bad news but our ingenuity doesn't stop there. Nowadays many of us feel like guilty slaves to our lust for sweets. We want to look sweet too and so with a little more human ingenuity we made our empty calories even emptier. With minimal compromise (who said there's no free lunch?) we've got calorie-free.

Sometimes it bothers us, this capacity of ours to design virtual experiences that rival the real ones. We try out various postures to make ourselves comfortable with the ersatz arts: We say there's nothing like the real thing; that people will soon come to their senses and demand authenticity; that when you cross a certain unspecified line (for example, with breast implants) you're amoral, which is to say that the other side of this alleged line, make-up and figure-flattering clothes are fine.

These virtual technologies are eroding our resolve to keep it real, but in other ways they are forcing us to get more real. Take a fairly basic virtual technology: writing. Writing is like a virtual memory bank, but one that reads like an open book. When an author puts ideas on paper, they are requisitioned out of memory to be spliced into cohesive sentences, paragraphs, and chapters. It then becomes much harder for the author to selectively mix and match them, never juxtaposing conflicting ideas. Even if the author is loath to note an inconsistency, his or her colleagues will provide that service. Authors and readers are virtually contracted to be each other's continuity experts, and on paper they have tangible evidence to work with in determining where the right hand doesn't know what the left hand is doing. It may be that science was an inevitable outgrowth of writing.

Through writing the selective pressure for internal consistency became a more important criterion in selecting what to believe. That's a scary thing about writing. It is also why so many writers say that they write to discover what they really think. By spilling the content of your mental inventory onto paper you surrender some of your ability to control which of your ideas meet each other.

In sum, we obviously benefit from some combination of make-believe and real-world reality checking. We can identify circumstances in which the human capacity to hope or the human capacity to face reality serves us well, and other circumstances in which the hope and reality checks get us in trouble. We can see that with science and technology we're harvesting some hybrid combination of dreaming and facing reality, as though science stumbled onto some extremely useful rules for toggling between dreaming and facing what is. And with what this combination provides us—all the new ersatz arts, the line between real and fantasy gets harder to draw.

174

Dream vs. Reality

How it shows up:

If dreaming, then do plan A.

If facing reality, then do plan B.

Getting it wrong:

False positive: Facing reality when dreaming would be better.

False negative: Dreaming when facing reality would be better.

Too sure: Assuming you're getting the right mix of dream and reality when you aren't.

Too unsure: Wondering whether you've got the right mix of dreaming and reality when you do.

Whirrings at Night:

People say I'm a dreamer. But am I the only one?

They say it's already been tried, but how do they know how many times it has to be tried before it succeeds?

I can't stand him. He'd chew off his leg to escape the bear-trap of reality.

Why should my son die in a war waged by our delusional leader?

Maybe it is time to get a real job. I'll never be a successful writer.

What they'll call you, if you:

	Live dreams	**Face Reality**
Prove Right	Visionary Optimistic Entrepreneurial	Practical Down to earth Realistic
Prove Wrong	Over-optimistic Out of touch Clueless	Unimaginative Pedestrian Uncreative

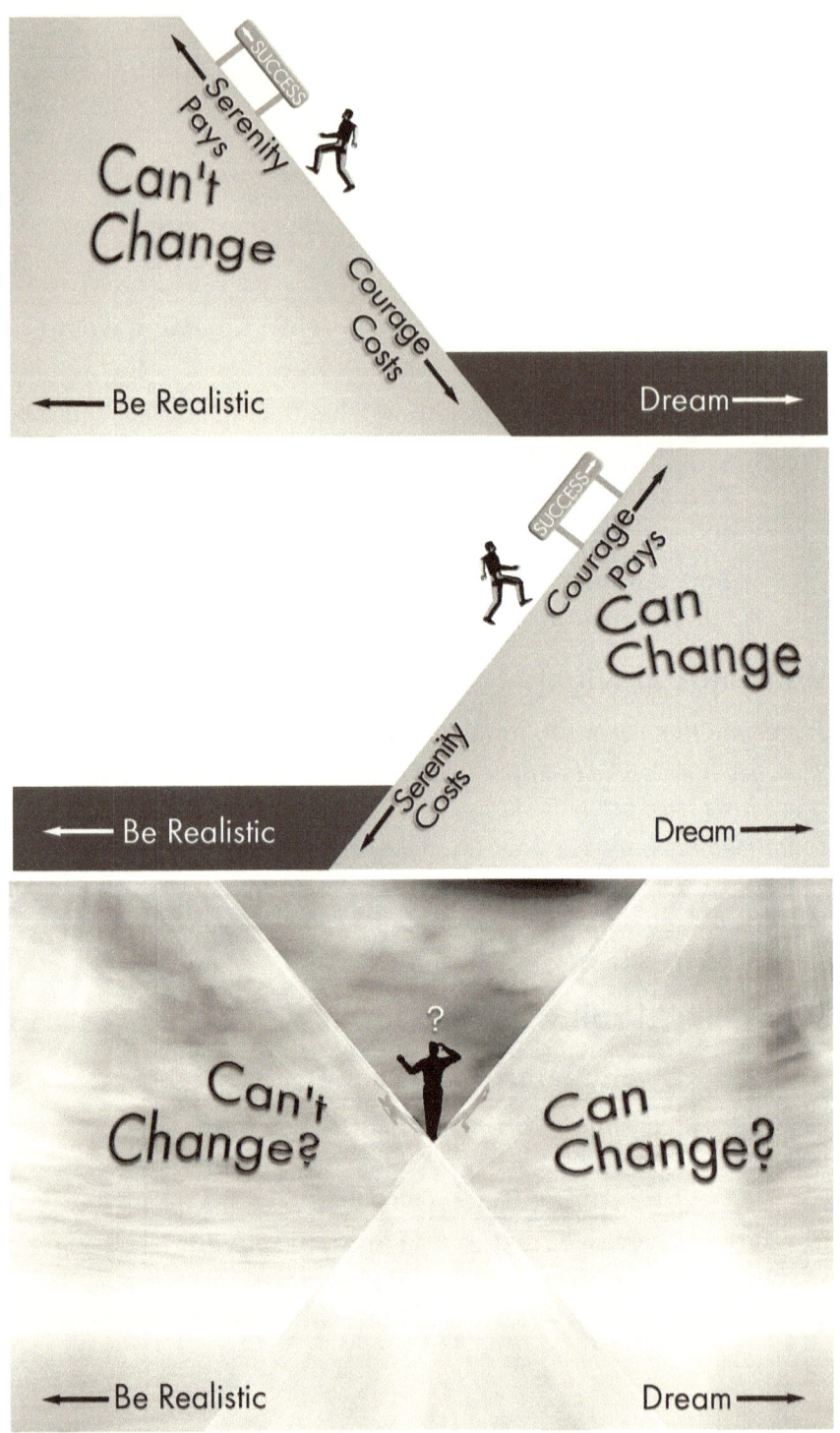

Just fork-edit:

'Be a Realist'

'Live your dreams'

Imagine how hard life would be if you could take stock of all facts and all memories at once. It's probably a good thing that you are spared seeing it all pass before your eyes until your last moments of life. It would be so overwhelming that it would shorten life considerably.

Our limited scope is a wonderful thing. It enables us to toggle between realism and dreaming. When you've already decided to accept something as it is, you can remind yourself that it is always best to be realistic, and conversely, when you've already decided to commit to changing some aspect of reality, it may be helpful to remind yourself that it's always best to live your dreams. And with limited scope we never need to see the comings and goings of our absolutes.

Most of us can't help but see the persistently problematic tension between realism and dreaming in our own lives. Most of us at one time or another have experienced impostor syndrome— the sense that we might be kidding ourselves. What do we do with persistent problems? According to the fourth wondering, we either ignore them and hope they go away, or confront them and hope they go away. One way to ignore them is to disavow them. Come out strong in opposition to kidding-oneself. Pledge yourself to never do it again. Eschew it and hang out with others who do too. The pledge may help keep delusion away, but not necessarily. Swearing off delusion is not the same thing as effectively purging it. It may be a successful way to pretend it purges it. The realist, when confronted about a spot of self-delusion he missed, is armed and ready to claim, 'There must be some mistake. I'm a realist and would never delude myself."

The alternative, taken to extremes is to face the persistence of delusion, admit it publicly and try to make friends with it, "Sure I delude myself. We all do. Life is but a dream. At least I'm not boring and mired in the mundane."

177

Take It Personally (T.I.P.)

No matter how hard I chase the truth, it will never catch me.

You might get the impression from all that you've read so far that this book is advocating a position of harsh realism: Face facts. Recognize that you delude yourself, and you should just stop it. Meet all dilemmas with healthy doubt and skepticism. Never fork-edt. Always keep uncertainty firmly in mind.

This is a somewhat popular notion these days in some circles. We're all making up our reality. We say we want the truth, but really we are trying to avoid it. We construct our reality and peering behind the veil we see all the jury-rigging and make-do scaffolding, which are easy to deconstruct. This doctrine of deconstruction is right on time—a perfect antidote to science's early dreams of becoming the supreme arbiter of reality. It is a product of science's success. Skepticism has been good for us in recent years. Doubting the prevailing truths enabled science to uncover facts about the way things work that have proven very useful indeed. It's no wonder that we've taken skepticism to its logical extreme, all the way to a kind of cynicism.

Call it the doctrine of foregone inconclusion: "If we can't ever get beyond our feeble mind-set construction kit, we can't really ever know what is true. Science, since it too is constrained by its own theories, is no supreme authority. No conclusions are ever absolute and given this foregone inconclusion, I'm going to believe whatever I want."

Wanting to believe anything is evidence that the tension between skepticism and belief is not easily overcome. We both chase the truth and try to avoid its inconveniences, all of us—even scientists. And though you never can tell, you will die trying, because though there are no certainties, some bets are better than others.

The Sixth Wondering of the Modern World:

Should I Say It?

You're having lunch with a friend who asks you what's new. You answer with enthusiasm. Most people really enjoy this opportunity to talk about what they're up to, bringing our news to the table with such eagerness that we compete for airtime. At other times, we're reluctant to share. What's this attraction and aversion about? Why share, and why resist sharing?

Telling your story is a chance to revisit your plans, goals, and aspirations and get them re-enforced and/or critiqued. The "and/or" is the sixth wondering of the modern world: We want two things—affirmation and feedback. But at least sometimes, the two work at cross-purposes to each other, so we wonder which to go for, and, as a listener, which to give.

A friend's approval of your story will have you up from the table pumped with high resolve. The light of support they shine at you dries up excess doubt. But it's a gamble, at least with some lunch mates. When they challenge us it breeds more doubt. A second opinion can make us lose our stride, which could be a good thing if we're striding in the wrong direction. Sometimes their critique is just what the doctor ordered, even if we would prefer a clean bill of health.

The sixth wondering is a direct extension of many wonderings that preceded it, going back to the first wondering of the ancient world—what company to keep; what company to avoid. It goes back to our friends Lax, Ox and Axe, and the different kinds of value that they bring to the table, encouraging us to try something new, to stay on course, or to be more discerning. It goes back to what you can and can't change about someone—when is feedback worth giving and when is it a waste of breath since they aren't going to change anyway? It relates to what you should and shouldn't air. It's about your role as a selectrician, consciously or unconsciously picking the company you keep at least to the extent you have any control over the matter. This sixth wondering is a thoroughly modern wondering, arising with our unique capacity to make mental movies starring the self, and then to project these movies on other people's mental movie screens so they can view them and share their views with us.

179

The two distinct benefits to sharing our stories with others are sometimes completely compatible, for example, when a friend's honest second opinion is that you are right on track. But when a friend sees flaws in your thinking, the ambivalence kicks in: You said we wanted feedback but you were hoping it would be a little more affirming. It doesn't work to say 'I want feedback so long as it's affirming,' because it wouldn't feel affirming if held to that condition.

It's guesscrow all over again: To tap into the unspecified amount in universe's escrow account of support for your plans (as channeled through your lunch mate) there's no alternative to sticking your neck out, declaring your commitments, and seeing what comes of it.

Why do we need the approval in the first place? We humans are extremely social animals. We bring to our relationships the obsessed attentiveness of eagerly devoted dogs, but the tricks we do to get approval are much more elaborate than a dog's. We can match mental movies with those whose approval we want, becoming almost brainwashed to win them over. Isn't that a mistake? Shouldn't we be more independent?

Sure, there's probably some personal and psychodynamic reason why any and every one of us is particularly needy or into pleasing or, alternatively, busy rebelling against being needy or pleasing. But beyond the details, we care what others think for solid practical reasons.

None of us can see everything from every angle. Other eyes help us see and know what to do, so it's worth paying attention to what other eyes see and other minds think. We are lucky to have this capacity to talk things out over lunch. It affords us the ability to learn vicariously from each other's experience. It's the key innovation that enables us humans to innovate and create the very fancy world we've created, a world so rich in things to learn that there's no way that a human being could come up to speed in it without being able to borrow from each other's minds. Think of the knowledge that we've accumulated over the past few hundred years. Even one hundred years ago it was possible for a scholar to read every book within his or her field. Now that would be impossible. Think of what slow learners we'd be if we couldn't take each other's words for things, for example, if we had to all go through the trial-and-error process of inventing everything that's ever been invented.

We humans are born more receptive to learning from experience than other creatures, but before we've accumulated experience ourselves, we borrow our parent's accumulation. We borrow their experiences through our appetite for doing the things that make them smile affirmingly and through our aversion to earning their frowns and scorn.

Approval-seeking later in life isn't just some carry-over of childish ways. We need affirmations because it's hard to stick with a plan, especially these days. We rely on others to help us find our way among our many options, which beckon to us from every street corner. To withstand the gusts of diversion and distraction, we need help. When people affirm our commitments, they're loaning us a sandbag to help us keep our commitments from blowing away. When they give us feedback they are usually trying to help us nudge our commitments to what they guess is safer ground, in spite of all the sandbags we've already piled on top of our commitments to keep them from moving. Our lunch mates are our sieves. That we care about successfully meeting their standards motivates us to make good plans. But caring as much as we do, we can be reluctant to hear their critique. It's a fine line.

There are a few common dance moves people make along this fine line—toggles that enable us to play both sides of it. One is a variation on the dance we've already seen and described as "the misinterpretation of tats." Your friend tells you his news. He ends a sentence or two trailing off with, "I don't know . . . " As a fairly sensitive listener, you intuitively assess this as a sign that he is open to feedback and you have some. As a fairly diplomatic friend, you say it as nicely as you can. You start with something affirming. You deliver the feedback as room for growth not as a shortcoming.

But in spite of your efforts, you friend doesn't receive the feedback the way you meant it and it turns out he brought to the table some antibodies against discouraging feedback however encouraging it was meant to be. It turns out his "I don't know . . ."s weren't so much a sign of receptivity to feedback but rather as evidence of his own ambivalence, and now that you've given him an opening, he can create a simple division of labor: You be the doubter; he'll be the defender. It's a preservationist move. He's trying to maintain his conviction, which is innocent enough, but the consequence is somewhat insulting—he discounts your feedback, implying that you're jealous or simply going to take his vulnerability as an opportunity to one-up him. Of course, if that's your motivation, there's no reason he should take it lying down. Two can play that game. It's a good thing he went first. Now when you tell him your plans, he'll be more critical since that's apparently the standard here.

Tit for tat. But, how can we know whether it really was a tat? You don't remember attacking, so his retaliation feels like a first strike. Your motivation was honorable in giving the feedback. You did your utmost to make it positive. A lot of thanks you get for sticking your neck out. . . .

We can carry around antibodies to neutralize unwanted feedback or we can pre-screen the sources of feedback so that we only share with people who are on the same page as we are. But how narrowly do you want to pre-screen? We celebrate diversity, but for practical purposes it's best to ally with people who share your values. You wouldn't want to get cloistered in some narrow homogenous community of yes-men and yes-women. You want friends who support you, but you don't want some mutual admiration society in which everyone is humoring and supporting everyone else just as a way to get the support they need. Mutually assured deconstruction: "I promise I won't critique your story if you don't critique mine."

The company we keep has a direct effect on our goals and therefore on the size of our aspirational gap. Their presence is both a carrot and a stick, pulling and pushing us to close the gap. Like all carrots and sticks they can be motivating or de-motivating. A friend who, by example, holds you to a high standard entices you to emulate that standard, but if the standard is too high, it's de-motivating. A friend whose goals are on par with yours or lower can be very affirming. In that friend's company, you feel the pleasure of a closed gap, which can encourage you to set even higher goals for yourself or can make you complacent, resting on the laurels your friend reminds you that you have.

When a friend provides us with critical feedback we face tough choices: Should we heed their warnings or pick new friends? You wouldn't want to take to heart feedback from someone whose perspective is no longer useful. Nor would you want to close your ears to it, and to the bearer of it, just because the feedback is discouraging.

The better you are at not being the best, the better you get to be. Finding teachers, bosses, and mates who are in our league but in the upper range of it can bring out the best in us. If you have the talent and gumption to meet the standard they represent, closing the gap by legitimate means, then a bigger gap can accelerate your learning. Of course if one doesn't mind being around people who are much better than they are because they don't care, or because they delude themselves that they are on par with the company they keep, then not being the best is not really an opportunity for growth. You've got to care what other people think for their standards to make a difference.

Still, there's always a risk in this reliance upon each other as standard-bearers. People's standards shift. Someone you've relied upon for affirmation can suddenly become the source of critical judgment you don't want, but can't help but absorb, because you've already subscribed to them as your designated goalkeeper. The danger has only grown in recent centuries as we've generated all of these new lifestyles and high standards for what constitutes success. It's hard enough to find someone who spells success the way you do, and it is very likely with all the options available to us that, over time your standards will shift in different directions. Your old business partner, or spouse of fifteen years—you shared values long ago, but now you've changed. People change and the galactic tugs you have relied upon from them can shift you in the process. If you are caught unawares, you can find yourself trying to meet the standards of a person whose standards are no longer relevant to you. You can find yourself trying to extricate yourself from a habituated commitment to pleasing or impressing someone who's angry with you for moving away and demands to know why you are disrupting such a long-standing commitment. Often when we shift values it's not by drifting but by 180-degree turning. Suddenly a former ally becomes the representative of all you are now turned against. Shifts like these can be very painful.

Remember that throughout we've been talking about doubts which were originally defined using the acronym A.C.I.D.S. The I.D.S. stood for "implying divergent solutions" and this has implications for the sixth wondering and the company we keep. A lot of the company we keep is made up of people who share a common standard for success. When we collaborate with these people, we are either working to get things done according to plan or thinking through some aspect of the plan, wondering together what to do. When we're wondering together, chances are good it's about some A.C.I.D.S., and since the cues are ambiguous and the solutions divergent, we can easily find ourselves negotiating in very black and white: one of us advocating one solution, the other advocating the divergent or diametrically opposed opposite solution. The fact that you two are on the same page, working on the same goal, actually means you are more likely to be on opposite sides of an issue more than you would be if you were concentrating on different goals altogether. Whether or not opposites attract, it is easy, when attracted to the same goal, to find yourselves on opposite sides. And then what? How strong should you ally? How much should you go along to get along? How much should you share your honest feedback?

Truth vs. Care

How it comes up:

If cue X then say what I really think.

If cue Y then juts be supportive.

Getting it wrong:

False positive: Giving feedback when affirmation would be better.

False negative: Giving affirmation when feedback would be better.

Too sure: Assuming it's one or the other when you'd do well to wonder.

Too unsure: Doubting whether you've read it right when you have.

Whirrings at Night:

I don't know why I bother giving him suggestions. He's not listening anyway.

Why was I codependent for so long? I've enabled her and now she's a disaster. I should have put my foot down long ago.

I'm so bored with them. How can I tell them we've grown apart?

She won't change until she gets away from those people. They bring out the worst in her.

What they'll call you if you:

And they:	Share truth	Show care
Like what they got	Helpful Challenging Tell it like it is	Kind Supportive Affirming
Didn't like it	Unkind Hypercritical Judgmental	Humoring Yes-man Afraid

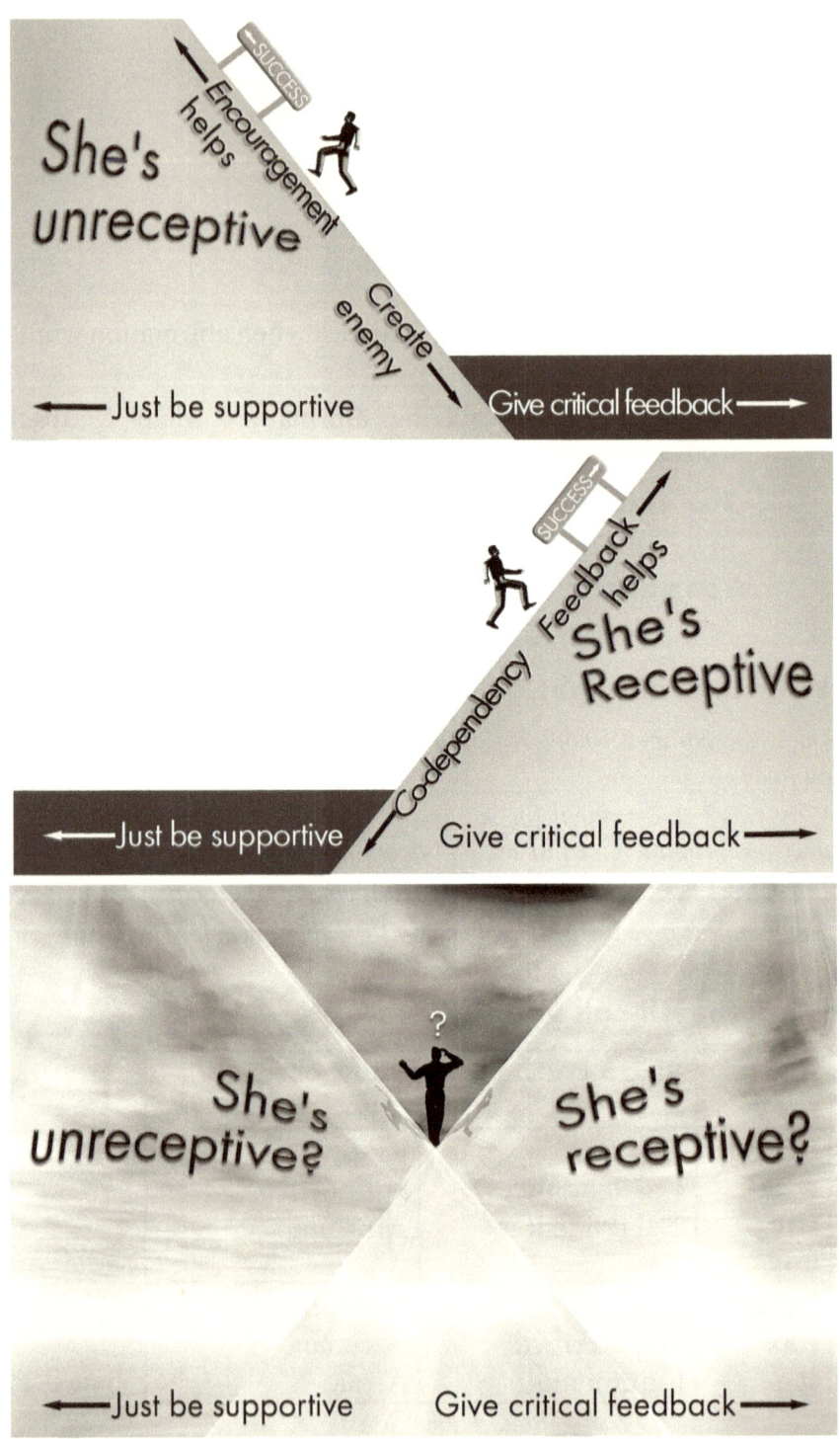

Just fork-edit:

'I just want the truth'

'If you don't have anything kind to say don't say anything at all'

There's nothing wrong with wanting both truth and care. The problems arise when we pretend we only want one to the exclusion of the other. "I just want the truth" has that telltale word, "just" in it—a disavowal of the basic human need to get a little affirmation for what we are doing even at the expense of truth.

Your friends share many assumptions with you. The basecoat of friendship is affirmation—having someone who perceives things the way that you do. You may want your friend's honest opinion, but that's because your friends are preselected for their similarity to you, so their honest opinions will be in the same ballpark as yours.

Lurking in the back of our minds always is a sense that outside our circle of friends and our accumulated beliefs about the way things work, there's some factor we haven't thought of, some spoiler of an idea that throws everything or anything we know into question. This possibility is a real and perturbing problem that won't go away, though we can make the feeling of doubt it engenders go away by circling the wagons, in effect, creating immunities to doubt in the form of strong-minded friends who will support you through thick and thin.

Paradoxically, one of the best antibodies to doubt is the declaration that we welcome it, claiming to be realists, not the least bit afraid of facing the truth. A lot of conversation among friends is analysis of the cluelessness of others outside our circle as though they are fundamentally less receptive to reality checks than we are. The contrast makes us think that we on the inside are safe because we, unlike these other people, welcome what's on the outside and are not afraid to consider any doubt. Claiming this kind of supreme receptivity is like announcing that you've already taken stock of outside perspectives and thereby neutralized anything lurking out there that might have caused us to doubt. To make this antibody work we don't have to be willing to consider any doubt. We just have to appear to fearlessly open, wanting the truth above all.

The ideal belief is one that feels comfortable and smells scientific. An unbiased assessment proves that my biases are correct. A dream come true is to relax into exactly who you are, and have the world affirm it. Few of us are fortunate enough to have the whole world affirm who we really are. The closest we come is to have a circle of friends who affirm us.

And when we've come to expect a friend to affirm us and one day he doesn't, we can either absorb the doubt our friend's dis-affirmation generates or discredit the friend. There are handy pseudo-moral sentiments we can draw upon when necessary that imply that the friend's dis-affirmation is some kind of failure of character or misbehavior on his or her part. "If you don't have anything kind to say, don't say anything" was a more credible moral sentiment a few decades back, but it still blows a strong enough gust to dispel a friend's challenges to our beliefs if we call upon it to do so. And if not with this universal rule then with some other one. A classic is "you're being judgmental," whatever that means—as though there were some natural or moral law that we should not experience or ever declare preferences for one bet over another. Preference predates consciousness. It is as old as life itself and the lifelong pursuit of better bets, which entails some equivalent of judgment—assessing situations and behaving differently in different situations.

Take It Personally (T.I.P.)

A save in time stitches nine.

By acknowledging that we come to the table wanting truth and care—two ideals that sometimes run at cross-purposes to each other, we recognize that misunderstandings can and will happen. There will be times when your friend will snappishly retaliate against your challenges when you really meant no harm, and the same in reverse can happen too. It is therefore worthwhile to do what we can to keep from jumping into battle with each other, but more importantly to learn how to de-escalate. Sometimes we can't avoid a mishap, but we can perfect the "save."

De-escalating fights with friends and colleagues takes stepping outside yourself a little, getting agnostic enough about who is right or wrong to simply declare that you don't know. One thing you do know is that there is a fundamental pattern of interaction that leads two parties to think that the other started it. Next time you find yourself in one of these battles (and you will), try reminding your friend (opponent) that together you've fallen into the oldest and most common conflict-trap there is—tit for tat when it's not clear whether there was a tat.

No two of us are compatible on all fronts. The compatibility that counts most is in how you deal with incompatibility. Being good at de-escalating will stitch up the inevitable rifts that grow between any two people.

The Seventh Wondering of the Modern World:

How Should I Know Myself?

You're sitting in a movie theater—a real one this time—and you're thoroughly absorbed in the drama unfolding before you, competently interpreting the characters' actions and motives.

The guy two seats down from you gets up and shuffles through your aisle to get out. For a moment, his logistics become your problem, popping you out of the drama on the screen and into awareness of the darkened theater. You see yourself along with two hundred strangers, including the one with unusually big hair sitting in front of you, all watching virtual reality—lights flashing on a white screen. The movie loses some of its power. The aisle clears again and you're right back, absorbed in the drama.

Now switch theaters: You're watching your life's drama unfold in your mind's eye and you're following the action closely, competently interpreting the player's actions. Many of the players are interesting, but by far the most absorbing character is you. Occasionally though, something shifts, and you catch a glimpse of yourself watching and interpreting. For a moment—just a moment—the drama loses some of its power.

When should you stay engrossed—unquestioningly interpreting your life's drama—and when should you step back to question your interpretation? When is it best to let the interpretation accumulate automatically and when is it best to examine your process of interpretation? That's the seventh wondering of the modern world.

It's about the stories we tell ourselves about ourselves, the mind's eye movies in which we are the central character. They are a uniquely human source of self-governing guidance. We can imagine lots of alternative scenarios for ourselves—different scenes and different interpretations of them—but we don't explore just any alternatives. We've got business to take care of, decisions to make and bets to place. So we search for, and latch onto, interpretations that we can really sink our mind's eye teeth into.

Honing to a fine and narrow point the movies we run about who we are and what we're doing is of great benefit. When you run a story that sticks, you focus your limited attention on a few good bets, which is about all you really have time for anyway in this life.

When you can say, "I am a professional cook, devoted parent, and adoring spouse, who loves dogs, and plays in local Scrabble tournaments"—and when you can really mean it—you increase your odds of being that person you describe, and that person isn't a bad thing to be.

Still, why not a scientist? Why not single? Why not cats? Why Scrabble? Why not chess?

Don't ask. Questions like these diffuse your focus. It's your story and you're sticking to it.

A single solid story about who you are is a selective filter on your behavior. Some option comes along and you can compare it quickly to what you know yourself to be. "No, I'll pass. Adoring spouses don't do that." Never underestimate the power of a strong yarn to tie yourself down to good bets. The catch is that a strong yarn can tie you down to bad bets too. So you need to slacken the yarn every once in a while. But when?

Just as in our friendships we need a combination of affirmation and critical second opinion and in biology we need a combination of R-Retention and V-Variation, in our storytelling we need a combination of firmness and flexibility, conviction and receptivity. There will be times for both, but the seventh wondering is which one when? They are both necessary, but they often operate at cross-purposes to each other. The more conviction you've got about your identity, the less receptivity to becoming something else. The more receptivity, the harder it is to maintain conviction. Conviction is forward thrust, like gas to your engines. Receptivity is the capacity to steer. If you are all conviction, you move but sometimes straight into obstacles at high speed. If you are all receptivity, you could maneuver around obstacles if you ever got to any, which is unlikely because you're just idling around in circles.

Conviction is like exhaling, putting out, asserting an interpretation. Receptivity or doubt is like inhaling, refreshing, and updating the mental movie screen with alternative imagery. Just as you can't breathe in and out at the same time, you can't be full of conviction and receptivity at the same moment. This fundamental tension between conviction and receptivity is what the ancient masters had in mind when they talked about yin and yang. Yin is openness and receptivity. Yang is conviction—the sword of decisiveness. "I play Scrabble. NOT chess."

How does one get receptive? The answer to this is changing. In the old days receptivity was a product of docility, an extension of the childlike deference to higher authority—king, priest, husband, master, boss. Your story about who you are could indeed change, but primarily because the authority made you change it, or changed your circumstances so drastically that you toggled to a new unexamined version of who you are.

Cultures around the world are gradually growing up, which is not necessarily a good or a fun thing, but this simply means that, increasingly, people have the freedom and burden of picking and choosing among authorities. Now increased receptivity is a matter of shopping for a better story, and deciding when you need one and when you should just stick with the existing one. Lots of versions of who you could be; lots of versions of how to decide. Once you've popped your head outside of your interpretation of the engrossing drama you're in, it gets harder to believe that your interpretation is the only one possible. Increasing numbers of us are no longer Version Virgins, and the question becomes like the old song title: How do you keep them down on the farm now that they've seen Paree?

The new receptivity is made possible by the capacity to see yourself in the theater watching the movie: Close your eyes and you can picture yourself closing your eyes and picturing yourself— a trivial exercise, perhaps, but one with huge implications for how we make decisions. Increasingly, receptivity is a function of this strange human ability to notice yourself in the theater, to examine your process of interpretation, stepping out of the drama to see yourself absorbed in it. It's a new trick, only a few thousand years old. It is the birth of second-guessing.

To put this new form of receptivity in context, a little update to the natural history of wondering is in order here. We had four acts and now we'll add a fifth.

To recap, in acts one and two instinct and pleasure and pain— the neural equivalents of do and don't— guided behavior. No
192

Introspection. No self-interpreter. No "I." We could call it I^0. I to the zeroth power. At I^0, there's no I. The I stands for "I" the self, for Introspection, or self-Interpretation—none of these are operative at I^0.

Plants, plankton, and potato bugs—and billions of other organisms—live entirely at I^0. They have behavior; some of them have neurology. They have behavior, but they don't have an inner interpreter of their own behavior. In that sense you could say that a movie is playing on the screen, but there's no movie watcher.

According to the peculiar laws of math, anything to the zeroth power is one, and indeed I^0 is the big unified oneness of life. It's a capacity we all have in common. Doing without knowing is the status quo state—the dominant mode of life. Though we humans are capable of more than it, we too rely heavily on I^0. Your skin exfoliates, your heart ticks, your lungs breathe, your liver purifies blood, all without requiring one whit of "I-ness." I^0 is also like I/O, which in computer science stands for input/output. At I^0, living things are simply input/output devices, taking in cues and outputting behaviors.

In acts three and four of our natural history of wondering, we saw the emergence of mental movie making. In act three, movies of things other than the self, which to self-referential creatures like us is hard to imagine. You'd think the first mental movies would be vanity flicks, but no. While we can't be certain of what goes on in mind's eye of a non-human, the indications suggest that the movies do not contain much self-reference if any at all. Instead the show plays like those 3-D virtual reality games in which you don't see the character you are; but rather, you see through that character's eyes looking out at the threats and opportunities. That kind of observer-less observation is probably what a frog, dog, or cat sees in its mental movies.

In act four we turned the mental movie making inward, to include the self as its central prop or character. Here, I^1 is born. I^1 is "I," or introspection to the first power, basic introspection— the running, unexamined interpretations that accumulate in your mind's eye, for ready reference in deciding what to do next. It's the part that knows you are a Scrabble and not a chess player. I^1 is that internal someone who watches and interprets the I^0 behavior playing out on the movie screen. The interpretation that accumulates at I^1 is anything that has brain Velcro—all the news that fits, feels affirming, proves useful, is consistent with what you already believe, helps others figure out what to do with you, helps others like you more, and, of course, to some extent reflects your reality. Especially useful are those reliable interpretations that help you keep fresh your moments of high resolve, especially when your high resolve is called into question providing the ballast that we've discussed, the sandbags we drop atop our plans, expectations and goals to hold them down keep them from blowing away.

So now, act five: It was probably only a matter of time. Sooner or later a creature that can watch itself act and interpret its own actions would gain the ability to watch itself in the very act of watching itself; the ability to interpret itself interpreting. Call this I^2, Introspection squared, the capacity to examine the unexamined narrative.

Though there have been inklings of I^2 in philosophy for a few millennia, in practice it is relatively new, and in the grand scheme of life's search for guidance in dealing with the wonders, it is still-has-a-price-tag-on-it-new. It is highly influential in guiding us through doubts and decision making, but in the grand scheme of things the jury is still out on it. It is the birth of second-guessing, of awareness of internal ambivalence; it can lead to navel contemplation and can make people more independent and selfish. It is the source of the new flexibility that makes us extremely different from other animals.

I^2 has grown more prevalent in the last few centuries and has really been coming into its own in the last few decades. Why? For many reasons, but science and technology are at the root of a lot of them. Here are a few:

- Science has been hugely successful at solving practical problems. As a result its method seeps into all areas of culture. Science began as an effort to get the observer's interpretation out of the way, which you wouldn't even think of doing unless you knew the observer was interpreting.

- Of course, people have always suspected other people of interpreting reality, since the first lie, since the origins of the specious, since one person first noticed that another person didn't appreciate a fact that "should be obvious to any clear thinking human being." It is quite a leap, however to turn skepticism inward upon oneself.

- And of course, people have probably long been able to look into their pasts and say, "Yes, I interpreted wrong in that instance," but it is a far rarer thing to assume that interpreter's bias is a universal and systemic problem from which none of us are exempt. That is the assumption that science most successfully codifies.

- Science rests on the assumption that you can never put it past any of us to interpret the world through distorting lenses. Science is an attempt to establish systematic rules for minimizing the distortion. The scientific method, to the extent that it is employed, imposes constraints on anyone's and everyone's bias, including the most esteemed scientist. It assumes that people tell motivated stories. Instead of just going with the liked story, scientists try to move it out of the way long enough to discover the likely story. To do this, science puts interpretive bias on the table where one can keep an eye on it. As the scientific method spreads into all areas of culture, it promotes the I^2 perspective in which the observer is observed.

- Science works, and we have technology to show for it. With science's successes has come a culture of skepticism. Of course, we remain far better at administering healthy skepticism to other people's biases, but we live in a democracy where double standards are increasingly difficult to justify, so we can't help but look skeptically inward now and then, catching a glimpse of our own motivated storytelling, which is an I^2 move.

- Science and the technology that pours forth from it give us the power to travel and communicate globally, exchanging ideas with people of very different cultures from our own. Exposure to alternative perspectives calls into question the perspectives we formerly held as self-evident. Strangers look at us in disaffirming ways—more truth than care— more second opinion than we get from our fellow natives. Before communication technology took off, people mostly lived around people who believed as they did; strangers

195

were rare, and their unusual habits were therefore easy to dismiss. With persistent exposure to each other's weird ways, we can no longer dismiss alternatives as we used to. It becomes increasingly difficult to avoid seeing ourselves as others see us, even others who see us very differently. This causes us to examine our unexamined narratives.

- Science and technology lets us put our stories in physical form, printed matter, recording, the movies that play in real movie theaters. As a result, human storytelling has really taken off. A single telling can be heard by millions, not just by a few people around a campfire. Taking in as much fiction as we do gives us extraordinary watching and interpreting skills. We get to study other people's motives in such depth that it can't help but seep back as how we study our own motives.

- Science and technology update culture at an accelerating rate, not just through the latest information, but through the ever-growing accumulation. Today, there are more books, magazines, films, tapes, and web sites than there ever before, but nothing like the accumulation people will face in another fifty years. We are privy to a brainchild population explosion, and with so many options, it becomes harder to stick with one option for long. We have come to expect our current beliefs to be out-of-date in a few years. As the flood grows larger, the pinhole of consciousness feels smaller. The interpretive lens we've fashioned for the pinhole becomes more readily swept out to sea.

This also means that more of us today know what it is like to have abandoned a cherished assumption than ever before. For better or worse, and in a way that parallels the rising divorce rate, we are less wedded to our beliefs than people were in times past. Once you've abandoned one hard-and-fast belief and survived or even thrived without it, you know that you can. What's to stop you from abandoning other givens should they start to prove cumbersome? People who divorced once are more likely to do it again.

So is this extraordinary new ability to examine our own convictions a move toward higher consciousness? By our earlier definition of consciousness as seeing more of the whole, it has to be. An omniscient God would be able to picture everything, including Himself picturing everything. In this sense a person's move toward examining her own convictions is a move toward godliness.

Is it therefore a good thing? Not necessarily. Remember the potato bug. Most of life gets by quite satisfactorily with I^0 alone. On a need-to-know basis all of life, generally doesn't. It neither knows or needs to know what it is doing and why. Consciousness isn't the be-all and end-all. And even if it is a good thing one can have too much of a good thing.

Typically when we see a hierarchy like this from I^0 on up, we think higher is better. But there are benefits and costs to each of the levels of *I*-ness.

I^0 is efficient—efficient enough that 99.9999% of life relies on it alone. It's so efficient that we tuck as many useful learned traits into it as we can. We drive, play music and sports, eat, and otherwise operate as much as possible relying on the efficiency of low self-awareness. You don't have to keep telling the story that you are a cook and Scrabble player in order to live it. Instead, you tuck your sense of self into memory and let it and all the accumulated social reminders—your work schedule, Scrabble tournament dates, etc.— keep you on track. Only when something feels slightly amiss—for example, losing four Scrabble tournaments in a row— would you find yourself consciously reminding yourself and others that you play Scrabble and why. I^0 keeps you on track, but a little over-determined. It's not a state that engenders innovation. It makes you a creature of habit. Literally, a creature.

To get a feel for the downside of operating at I^0, consider a dog on a tangled leash. To untangle it, he needs to make a paradoxical move toward where it's tethered in order to get away. Most dogs can't get the hang of it, and it's the combination of things that make them I^0 that also make them incapable of making such paradoxical moves. Dogs can't step outside of their behavior to see their tangled selves in context. In a similar situation, you would act differently. Walking along in a blissfully I^0 state, thinking about nothing in particular, your coat snags. It catches your attention and your predicament rises to I^1 consciousness. You quickly picture yourself in context, figure out what has happened and untangle yourself by the paradoxical move of stepping toward the snag to free yourself to step away from it. I^0 is wonderfully efficient but not helpful for making the paradoxical moves that make humans so different. All I^0 and no introspection makes Jack a linear boy, unable to go into the red to get into the black.

I^1 is great for paradoxical moves. Tell yourself over and over that one day, you're going to be a great doctor, and you can endure the hardships of medical school, but I^1 storytelling can get you in trouble too. I^1 is like knowing yourself emphatically—the kind of introspection that enables us to say stubborn things like "Look, I know myself, and I'm not the kind of guy who would do a thing like that!" when in fact, you have.

I^2 enables you to examine your convictions, which has costs and benefits. It is good to doubt bad choices and bad to doubt good choices. We're glad that Gandhi dwelled as much as he did at I^1 with his firm unquestioned beliefs. We're sorry that Hitler didn't visit I^2 a little more often, examining his own convictions. I^2 may give you a bad case of conviction impairment but a healthy dose of flexibility endowment. I^1 will endow you with conviction but leads to flexibility impairment.

We have many terms for the act of introspection. For the most part, they cover the same territory, but some of them make it sound really bad and others make it sound really good. Self-knowledge is good, but self-consciousness is bad. Self-awareness is good, but self-obsession is bad. Self-examination is good, but self-doubt is bad. Self-esteem is good, but self-serving is bad.

This whole book is written as if from the observation deck at I^2, looking at the way we interpret our world of options. For example, throughout the book, we've been interpreting our "just fork-edits." These are the running unexamined interpretations we make of the way the world works.

Our just fork-edits don't hold up under I^2 examination. For example, it's dumb to make a decision based on the law that persistence always furthers, because it doesn't. But we've also come to recognize that, though "persistence furthers" is lousy data for decision making, it is extremely useful for decision-affirming. So, after having examined the story that "persistence furthers" and found it unsound, you may still want to use it, and other just fork-edits, to help you edit out of your mind the options you have decided not to take. That's the spin doctor's Hippocratic Oath, which really can only make sense to people who have the ability to pop out of their I^1 interpretations long enough to strategize about when and when not to rely upon them.

But this raises an interesting question: Once you've popped out I^1, can you ever get back in? Once you've noticed, for example, that "persistence furthers" is not always true, can you ever chant it convincingly to encourage yourself to stick with a project? Once you've arrived at I^2 is there any returning to I^1?

If exposing yourself to self-doubt is to begin a relentless process of unraveling, that may be reason enough never to pop out. Stay at I^0 and I^1. There are still plenty of people who never question their interpretations—whole nations of them. For people who don't examine their own assumptions, there's no good reason to visit I^2 and therefore there's no seventh wondering of the modern world. Many such people are very fine and productive, kind, strong, and, above all, reliable. Those of us stuck doubting ourselves sometimes envy them their self-certainty.

Still, some of these people are a pain. We abhor nothing more than the company of people whose interpretations are very much at odds with our own, and who can't or won't examine their interpretations. All of us do, but no one abhors their company more than other people who can't examine their own interpretations. Make dogmatists of different breeds live together and you could well be in for a hundred-year war.

The successes in this world are those who can keep a story fixed and foremost in their mind's eye for a long enough time to convert it from dream to realty. Or to put a finer point on it, the successes are those who can keep a *realistic* story fixed in their minds that long. The failures are those who are stuck obsessed on an unrealistic story—which is the reason to gain the flexibility to pop out to I^2.

Some of us who do pop out to an I^2 perspective pull back to I^1 as quickly as firmly possible. Forced by crisis to switch stories quickly, we can't help but notice for a moment that we have one. But the brush with failure that prompted us to examine our assumptions can be so terrifying that we avoid everything associated with it, including the vertigo of not knowing, of receptivity, of I^2 itself. A common move then, is to shift stories quickly, changing from Scrabble to chess, from devoted parent to delighted single, and promise ourselves never to be fooled again. Tell stories about how wrong the old story was and how right its replacement must be. Duck right back into I^1 and stay there. Done doubting, now and forever more. It's a move you could call, "I once was lost but now I'm blind."

A subtle version of this is to make I^2 the new state of certainty. Waking up to the benefits gained at I^2, some of us become doubt-chauvinists. The truth will always set us free, and since we're brave enough to face it, we know the real truth now. We frown upon self-deception, and then assume that disdaining it is the same thing as eliminating it. It isn't. Gaining the ability to observer our own convictions, we rush to accumulate convictions about our powers of receptive doubt: "I'm a no-nonsense pursuer of the truth, brave enough to face it." And then, "Look, I really know myself now, and I'm not the kind of guy who would delude himself."

For increasing numbers of us though, act five is succeeded by chapter six. Eventually we recognize with some disappointment that there are limits to our powers of receptivity and doubt, practical limits on what we can know and what we want to know.

It dawns on us that for every layer of story we tell, another story could be told about the teller of it. But who has time for introspection to the third, fourth, and infinite powers? We can imagine but not visit a state you could call *I*-ons, for I on and on and on . . . I^∞, introspection to the infinite power. If you had all the time in the world and infinite brainpower you could just keep on climbing to higher and higher nested crow's nests from which to look down on yourself observing yourself observing yourself. Instead of looking inward to find your true core self, the center of your being, you realize that every new true self you find at the center is actually another layer of story further and further out. Moving inward, you could reasonably hope to find a center point, but overlaying stories is as infinite as outer space. Layer upon layer. Only a god would be able to second-guess ad infinitum.

And ad nauseam . . . what happens to us when, in the back of your mind, lurks a constant reminder (typically the voice of your most deflating parental figure) that in your ever-limited self-interpretation you could well be missing something really big? Who wants to spend their time fishing for the one big catch they hadn't thought of—the one fact that changes everything? Start up that path and you are likely to catch some wonderful insights. But with exhaustive receptivity to insights comes exhausting doubt. A doubt that none of us can endure for long. So we button up. All of us do. There's work to be done. For every single insight into new possibilities, we are likely to experience at least two more pressing insights that you should get back to work, pay bills for the things you've already bought, feed your kids, feed the bets you've already made.

That's why even the most self-doubting among us strive for a balanced blend of affirmation and second opinion from our friends and a blend of conviction and receptivity in our inner lives. We mouth the merits of eternal receptivity to reality, but none of us can extend an infinite welcome to the juicy truths that could help us further refine our stories. We may wax philosophic about the yin-yang balance of receptivity and decisiveness, but when doubt is upon us, keeping us up at night, our curiosity wanes. We strive for peace of mind and a good night's sleep.

To obtain and maintain peace of mind, we keep on hand antibodies against doubt. Supportive friends are good. So are frequent visits to the movies where we can watch stubborn heroes persist against doubt and prevail with their long-shot bets. So too are the just fork-edits and other unexamined narratives that help us keep fresh our high resolve and blind us to alternatives we might have bet upon instead. I^1 is a gift and none of us are above using it.

It is a balance, nonetheless, and a somewhat treacherous one. The entrepreneur who can't step outside her convictions to wonder will be unaware of the oncoming impasses. The entrepreneur who can't help but step outside her convictions to wonder if she is doing it right will never get her venture off the ground. In order to pick our path we need receptivity. In order to progress on our path we need conviction.

The good news is that you can have both. Opening up to I^2 doesn't really render I^1 ineffective. Exposing yourself to your own interpretive bias doesn't mean bias is all that shapes your decisions, or that there's any alternative to bias. Bias is commitment to preexisting bets. None of us get a truly clean slate ever so none of us can ever bet without prior commitment. Conscious unconsciousness is possible. You can tell yourself unbelievable things, know that they are unbelievable, and still gain strategic benefits from telling them. For many of us who are conviction-impaired, having gained the versatility to pop up to I^2, we're glad we made it and we recognize increasingly that the trick becomes knowing when it's beneficial to do so.

Conviction vs. Doubt

How it shows up:

If conviction then do plan A.

If doubt then rethink.

Getting it wrong:

False positive: Standing by conviction when doubt is called for.

False negative: Rethinking when standing by conviction would be more effective.

Too sure: Never doubting.

Too unsure: Always doubting.

Whirrings at Night:

Am I on the right path?
Is something amiss?
I'm right. Why isn't the world responding the way it should?
Why are people so stupid?
They're against me, because I'm right and they know it.
I can't help but question my own motives, but doubting so much is making me ineffective.

What they'll call you, if you act from:

	Self-doubt	Self-certainty
Prove Right	Receptive Responsive Attuned	Decisive Focused Determined
Prove Wrong	Wishy-washy Weak-willed Impressionable	Pigheaded Closed-minded Tyrannical

Just fork-edit:

'Know thyself'

Know thyself is commonly taken to mean something like observe yourself, take the perspective outside thyself, and study your own nature. It can also mean knowing thyself in that unobserved way, as in, "I know myself and I'm not the kind of guy who would ever have a double standard!"

Both interpretations of "Know thyself" are useful self-admonitions. And they are opposites. Therefore, sometimes you need to know yourself, and other times you need to just know yourself. The trick is knowing when to do which.

Other admonishments addressed to selves can carry this double meaning also. "Get next to yourself" commonly means pull yourself together or step back into character, don't be so self-doubting, but it can also mean to step outside yourself onto the observation deck where you can witness yourself and question what you're doing, from a perspective outside yourself.

Either way these admonishments are addressed to the anxious self, maybe the ping-ponging self, perhaps the self who has committed to something and begins to doubt it. The anxiety that accompanies doubt is like a fork in the road. You either follow it into self-observation or resuming character. If you find yourself wondering whether you should quit your job, business, or marriage, or any other commitment because they feel hollow, you don't hear the bells ring or whatever, your choice is either to just fork-edit and resume (knowing thyself emphatically) or to question, step outside yourself, observe, and take stock, (knowing thyself inquisitively). So which is better?

It depends. Sometimes things feel bad and we howl, "There must be a better way." We drop out of character and take stock from a perspective that includes more possibilities than we normally assume possible. We stop saying, "How can I improve this?" and ask the wider question, "Can I improve this, and if not how do I get out, what else is there. I hope there's something better, maybe there's something better, there is something better, I've just got to go find it."

Declaring that there is something better is extremely useful to looking for it. If you know that there is, then all you have to do is find it.

Still there might not be something better, in which case you should resign yourself and get back into character. Staying out of character will inevitably make you forfeit that character. Spend too long in doubt about a relationship and soon that relationship will no longer be yours to consider.

The question is not whether self-perception is a good thing or a bad thing, the question is how much and what kind is good or bad.

Take It Personally (T.I.P.)

Not plain; Sweet and Sour.

By our age, we get it: Life is a balancing act. There's a time to laugh; a time to cry, a time to live, and a time to die, etc. etc. We're told to recognize the harmony in opposites. We are encouraged to step outside to an identity with one side of the balance or the other to appreciate the whole. This is good advice, up to a point. Your ability to get perspective on the balance of different forces is uniquely human and at the same time gives you a taste of a kind of equanimity nonhuman life seems to have. With less emotional or conceptual ballast tugging at them, other living things seem more at peace with the yin and yang harmony of it all than comes easily to us conflicted humans.

Balance sounds harmonious—the peaceful averaging of things. But that harmony is only apparent from the outside looking in, and you don't live there. You live inside your life where the balance of opposites rises to consciousness mostly when it's called into question and feels less like harmony than like ambivalence or ambiguity—an antagonism between opposites that both vie for primacy. Real tension, not some half-and-half blend, it's more like sweet and spicy than bland.

Stepping outside of the details of your life you can picture yourself kept aloft and buoyant by the multiple tugs that make up your mind, like a planet suspended and turning under the influence of gravitational pulls from many different forces. But sometimes that is not at all what it feels like. Your motives may not be fractional contributions that add up to one. When ambivalent, you are not half-heartedly drawn toward two things that can be tallied up to wholeness, but rather, wholeheartedly drawn in opposite directions. There's nothing to prevent life from being like that. There's no reason you can't want mutually exclusive things.

Sometimes you feel torn, pulled in different directions at once, not comfortable with the middle ground but wishing to fuse completely with irreconcilable opposites. Sometimes you can have your cake and eat it too, but then again, sometimes you can't, and these are when doubt besets you.

This may make life sound more dire, drastic, and discordant than you find it to be. As noted at the beginning and throughout, most of time we cruise in life. Why? We cruise because life has taken care of so many tough judgment calls already. The eons-old trial-and-error processes that have been sifting and integrating good guidance for tough judgment calls hum silently below consciousness, working so smoothly that you don't have to notice.

Our remaining stress is at the modern margins of doubt. Irreducible uncertainty, the stuff that no quantity of accumulated adaptive guidance will ever eliminate, conflicts between guidance gained—instincts vs. feelings vs. thoughts vs. culture, and the seven wonderings of the modern world that came with our new cognitive adaptive guidance systems. Being new-fangled, they aren't fully integrated with all of the other guidance we've got. They are bound to act up sometimes. The past few thousand years have released a particularly strong torrent of doubt for one species, and you, being a member of it, may at times find yourself weathering a lot of it. Take heart, and notice that you are right on schedule, not un-natural in

the least but rather one of nature's boldest bets.

T.I.P. Index

Jeremy Sherman

Suggested Reading

This book was based on current ideas in the academic fields of social psychology, cognitive science, decision theory, evolutionary biology, complexity theory and biological anthropology. For a complete bibliography visit 'www.evolvingpress.com/biblio.htm'. For suggested readings tailored to your interests, please contact the author at js@evolvingpress.com.

Gratitude

Either because people are generally wonderful, charming, generous, and encouraging, or because I have found and stuck with those who are with me, I have many to thank for seeing me through this consuming project. My gratitude to all whose names follow, first for the spurring and well-timed infusions of truth and care that, in the aggregate, made this book possible.

On matters of substance—the Darwinism, Taoism, and decision theory—I am grateful to Terry Deacon, Robert MacCoun, Alph Bingham, Ty Cashman, Bob Atkins, Jay Ogilvy, Ursula Goodenough, Amory Lovins, Doug Tucker, Matt Marlowe, Sandra Schneider, Barbara Smuts, Ed Scheuer, Harry Saunders, Peter Richerson, Frank Sulloway, Teed Rockwell, Owen Flannigan, and Daniel Johnson.

On the peculiarities of authorship and publishing my gratitude flows to my own brother Stuart Sherman, always a source of sustenance, and to Sheldon Bowles, Cheryl Simeone, Lynn Gordon, Fern Reiss, Dan Ellsberg, Bill Yenne, Amanita Rosenbush, Ron Schultz, Rosie Mestel, Meredeth Maran, Margret Mcbride, Phil Catalfo, Mary Schmich, Peter Leyden, Jay Levinson Susan Page and Kit MacCoun. I am also grateful to my editor, Dawn Adams.

For mutual muse-hood—comfort, love, and collaborative inventive conversation from which springs to birth so many insights—and in no defensible order, Lucy Sherman, Naomi Fine, Diane Malek, Maureen Whalan, Sara Boettiger, Adam Davis, Mary Lou Gifford, Laura Kennedy, Robert Seidenspinner, Margaret Hand, Sandra Cook, Alan Graf, Frank Poleti, Margaret Cook, Rasaki Aladokun and Steph Pamukoff.

For the pearls polished through illiquid thick-and-thin commitment, I owe much to my ex-wife Anne Hill, and my children Lucy, Will, and Alex; all of whom are serendipitous blessings.

And then, to my parents who begot, and got me wondering.